Practical Financial Management

THE SUNDAY TIMES

Practical Financial Management

7TH EDITION

A guide to budgets, balance sheets and business finance

Colin Barrow

KOGAN PAGE

Publisher's Note

Every possible effort has been made to ensure that the information contained in this book is accurate at the time of going to press, and the publishers and authors cannot accept responsibility for any errors or omissions, however caused. No responsibility for loss or damage occasioned to any person acting, or refraining from action, as a result of the material in this publication can be accepted by the editor, the publisher or any of the authors.

First Indian Edition 2010

Kogan Page India Private Limited
4737/23 Ansari Road,
Daryaganj
New Delhi 110 002

This edition is for sale in the Indian subcontinent only. Not for export elsewhere.

ISBN: 978-81-7554-483-3

Published by Vinod Vasishtha for Kogan Page India Private Limited,
4737/23 Ansari Road, Daryaganj, New Delhi - 110 002.

Printed and bound at Saurabh Printers Pvt. Ltd., New Delhi.

Contents

Part 2: Understanding the figures

Part 3: Figuring out the future

Getting the most from your business bank

What is it that SMEs look for in a business bank? Is it value for money or quality of service? The answer of course is both. By retaining the Business Moneyfacts Best Overall Business Bank accolade for the last 3 years, Bank of Scotland has firmly established itself as a major player in the business banking market.

SMEs have, for too long, received a poor deal from their High Street banking providers. With a combined market share of 80%, the Big Four High Street banks continue to enjoy a monopoly on the provision of products and services to SMEs. It is the most concentrated sector in UK banking and consequently, there is little incentive by these banks to improve the deal that they offer small businesses.

In recent years, Bank of Scotland has taken up this challenge of becoming the first British bank to bring consumer pricing to the business banking market. Offering both superior pricing on products alongside a first-class service to customers, Bank of Scotland is finally offering SMEs the deal that they deserve.

The best deal for business

Over the course of the last year, Bank of Scotland has revolutionised the business banking market by introducing a number of firsts for small businesses. In October 2007, we launched the market leading Total Business Account which offers an interest rate that is 4 times higher than is paid by any other bank. Another first saw the launch of the first ever offset account for business customers, giving businesses the opportunity to combine a Business Banking Offset Loan and a Business Banking Offset Account, potentially saving thousands of pounds on loan or mortgage repayments.

Customers switching over from the Big Four also benefited from their market-leading deals. SMEs switching over to Bank of Scotland from the competition saved nearly £8.3million last year. Under their Guaranteed to Beat proposition on their Business Current Account, they promised to pay out £1000 if unable to beat the business banking deal of any customer switching from the Big Four**.

Exceptional people sharply focused on their customers

It's not just well-priced products that small businesses are looking for their business bank to provide. Overall, small business owners would like to receive excellent value for money and a first class service from a bank that understands the financial requirements of their business. At Bank of Scotland, we pride ourselves on the quality of our people and the experience of business banking that we've built up over 200 years. The Bank invests heavily in its people, maintaining what is considered as the best team of Business Managers in the business. With expertise in business finance, our Business Managers deal with businesses of all types so they have a breadth of knowledge that's second to none.

Make switching a priority

Of course, there is still a huge amount of intransigence within the small business market – even from those businesses who are unhappy with their current providers. Research carried out by Bank of Scotland Business Banking showed that fewer than one in ten (8%) small business owners had moved their business bank account in the past three years. Just take a moment to consider whether you or your clients' current banking arrangements are giving you all you need to help your business. If the answer is 'No', why not switch to a bank that can support your business every step of the way?

* Source: Small Business Predictions research (Dec 07)

** This offer is available to customers who currently bank with Lloyds TSB, Natwest, Barclays or HSBC, have a turnover of £50,000 or more and are on a published tariff and not a free deal. Accounts are subject to status.

LOOK AT THINGS DIFFERENTLY

BANK OF SCOTLAND

In difficult economic times businesses need to find innovative and effective tools to provide growth and increase profit. Bartercard is such a tool and recently won Business Tool of the Year.

This prestigious award came from *Business Britain Magazine*, and is the latest in a long line of awards that have followed the impressive growth of Bartercard since its inception in Australia seventeen years ago.

Bartercard is the world's largest and fastest growing trade exchange with a worldwide network of more than 55,000 businesses, trading with each other in a vast array of products and services. It has its own currency called trade pounds and one trade pound equals one pound sterling.

Recently appointed UK Managing Director Tim Ashley Sparks says "Bartercard offers enormous advantages to businesses at any time, but when we experience poor economic conditions such as we are now facing, it comes into its own. Businesses – especially small to medium size businesses (SME's) – are always looking for a competitive edge, always have cash pressures and always have a strain on resources that constrains their ability to grow.

"What we do at Bartercard is to partner our members to help them achieve their short and long term objectives. With our local franchise offices working closely with the members we can deliver new customers and valuable new business giving the competitive edge that they are looking for, whilst at the same time reducing their cash expenses and thus improving cash flow."

If you were a business that needed to make purchases for the products or services that you use in the normal day to day running of your business, would you rather pay cash for these items or pay with your own product or service?

As an example, if a restaurant needs £1000 worth of printing and they are not part of the Bartercard network, they have no choice but to write a cheque for £1000. However, in Bartercard they could go to a Bartercard printer to receive the same product, price and service but when the printing was ready a simple voucher is completed which triggers the transfer of the 'payment' of £1000 trade pounds from the restaurants account to the printers account.

This means that the printer has been paid immediately – no bad debts – and the restaurant has received his printing having taken no cash out his business.

Now, the local Bartercard office works with both businesses – in the case of the restaurant, bringing in other Bartercard members as new customers. Every time these customers spend it reduces the debt for the restaurant, so as well as saving cash the restaurant has actually paid for his printing with food and drink, and £1000 worth of meals costs the restaurant much less than £1000.

On the other side, the printer can use his trade pounds instead of cash to purchase many of his normal overhead expenses. The result is two winners:

The restaurant has saved cash, gained new customers, and bought his printing for much less than the real value, whilst the printer has gained a new customer, been paid immediately, filled spare capacity and been able to save cash and reduce his day to day business spending.

Tim Sparks comments "one of the big problems for businesses in tough times is that they are forced to cut back on things that are even more important than in good times such as marketing, advertising and training. How much more of this essential spending could a business do if they were not having to use cash but were paying for such services with their own spare capacity. Not only can businesses increase promotional spend, but the resultant increased revenues are cash revenues therefore further enhancing their cash position."

Bartercard's UK business has over 5000 members in all business sectors and is growing rapidly. The model of local offices ensures that members are properly supported and members are allocated their own account manager to work with them as they develop and grow. Members can trade locally, nationally and internationally in any of the 18 countries that Bartercard operate.

Tim Sparks says "The UK can easily support 100,000 members so the opportunity for us is enormous. We have focussed the business on growth and are seeing the benefits every week. We have also recently reignited our drive to expand the franchise network and to this end we have recently appointed Brian Whitford MBE in the role of Business Development Manager to take responsibility for the sale of new franchises and the co-ordination of the marketing function. Mr. Whitford joined Bartercard at the end of 2004 as a franchisee, after a successful international business career. In the following three years he built his franchise to 500 members, so he has actually worked the model and is therefore perfectly placed to combine his previous experience with that of the Bartercard experience to ensure that we choose the right people to work with us to deliver the significant future growth that is our goal."

Brian Whitford commented "a Bartercard franchise offers the opportunity to build a large and successful business with all the benefits of having a major brand behind you and a dynamic and highly experienced central support structure. We offer an unparalleled support package to our franchisees and have the philosophy that we're in it together and in it for the long term."

If you would like to find out about membership or a franchise contact Brian Whitford on **0845-219-7000** or e-mail: **brian.whitford@uk.bartercard.net**

BARTER CARD

Preface

The long queues of depositors snaking around branches of Northern Rock, the investors, managers and employees of the collapsed Independent Insurance, once the ninth-largest insurance company in the UK, and the 25,000 or so self-employed businesspeople and companies that are bankrupted or put into liquidation each year have more in common than they might have thought. All were to a greater or lesser extent ignorant of or ill served by the accounts they should have been able to rely on to inform them of the safety and performance of the businesses concerned.

In the case of Northern Rock the over-dependence on a single source of finance and high gearing were the heart of the problem. For Independent it was the actions of a handful of directors attempting to disguise the true financial position of the company. The net effect of their 'window dressing' was that the annual accounts showed a £22 million profit rather than the loss of at least £180 million that was the true position.

For the tens of thousands of failed businesses the most common cause for closure is poor financial control. Indeed, surveys of businesses routinely indicate that a third of failures are accounted for in this manner. Directors and managers frequently leave financial questions to their accountants to sort out at the end of the year. They often have the mistaken belief that keeping the books is an activity quite divorced from the 'real' task of getting customers, making the product or delivering great service. By the time the figures are prepared by the accountant, most ailing businesses are already too far down the road to financial failure to be saved. Even the few businesspeople who do ask for advice, perhaps from an accountant or a bank manager, often do not understand the terms being used to explain the situation. The final accounts become all too final, and a good business proposition is ruined by financial illiteracy.

Financial Systems for Small Business –

Steve Farr, Microsoft Dynamics Product Marketing Manager

One of the key issues in describing or recommending systems for small businesses is arriving at a reasonable description of what a small business is. We could look at turnover, staff numbers and their skill levels or ownership: and any of these would tell us that there are a lot of small businesses in the UK. For example, The Department of Trade and Industry's Small Business Service takes a broad view of "fewer than 150 staff", and this yields 1.7 million companies employing 12.6 million people. (DTI, 2006). At Microsoft we use a measure of "fewer than 50 PC's", and this yields 1.2 million companies.

But both measures are crude, and as such hide the true nature of individual small companies. And unless we understand the needs of the individual small company we can not hope to suggest the IT systems most appropriate for running their business. Let's take two examples of small companies that would fit both definitions above.

Company A is a stationery distribution business based in and serving the Slough area. They have a stock list that runs to thousands of items and process up to 400 orders a day through 3 telesales staff. As well as managing stock levels their critical processes are in handling orders accurately, quickly and with price flexibility to meet customer expectations; and managing the delivery process with 3rd party logistics organisations so that they do not either under or over order capacity on any given day. Company A is part of a larger group with other locations in Swindon and Manchester. Each location runs autonomously but performance is compared between them. They employ a qualified accountant.

Company B is a plumber operating in rural North Wales. His customers are members of the general public spread over a broad geographic area. After a hard day on the road, bookkeeping consists of a pile of bills to pay suppliers and invoices to write to customers and post. The critical processes in this business are managing cash and ensuring that customers can get in contact and book appointments efficiently.

So how am I so confident that few in business have much of a grasp of financial matters? And, assuming that to be true, why should their ignorance matter?

Taking ignorance first: I'm sure you won't just take my word to prove my point, but I have sat in front of thousands of businesspeople whose eyes clearly glazed over as the merits of marginal costing were explained. But 'Did you actually test their knowledge?' would be a valid question to prove my point. Well, a couple of years ago I ran something we called the Business Brains Test. We invited businesspeople to take a series of short tests in various business subjects online and anonymously. Over a thousand did so, and the results were revealing.

The average score for the business public at large in the finance section of the quiz was 41 per cent, an absolute fail, and the results revealed some alarming areas of weakness. For example, nearly 80 per cent of those taking the test did not know what depreciation is. Over half could not make a rudimentary balance sheet calculation to show a business's borrowing requirements. This would indicate that many owner managers might not have any real idea what their accounts are actually telling them, particularly on matters of profitability.

I applied the same test to a control group of 168 people who had been through the Business Development Programme run at Cranfield over two years previously, so that any knowledge would not be too fresh. They scored 92 per cent, and so they should have; but did their scores matter a jot to the success or otherwise of their businesses? Well, according to the post-programme follow-up studies these companies:

- grew more than four times as fast – by 54 per cent compared to 12 per cent for privately owned businesses in general;
- doubled their return to shareholders;
- increased their profit growth at a much faster rate than prior to attending.

It is also true that successful, fast-growing businesses fail. But while the failures make the headlines and run to hundreds, tens of thousands of fast-growing businesses quietly prosper. Ask any receiver why businesses fail and he or she will almost invariably put lack of financial skills of the boss near the top of the list.

The message seems pretty clear. Finance is the language of business. If you learn that language and become more fluent you will improve your chances of business success and reduce your chance of failure.

This book is intended to help those who find business finance confusing. A heavy fog seems to descend as soon as anyone approaches this field for the first

Are you sitting comfortably?

Why ergonomic working is essential for even the smallest business.

Around 10.2 million working days are lost in the UK every year due to back, neck and upper limb problems.*

In the light of this uncomfortable fact, it's no surprise that the smartest businesses are increasingly realising the importance of creating a healthy working environment. Ensuring wellbeing at work – or *'wellworking'* as it's known, provides a wealth of benefits, including increased efficiency, better productivity and improved health. And whilst wellworking will help any business, it's particularly important for small businesses.

Why are small businesses so at risk?

Start-up businesses often don't invest in the right office furniture. These same businesses require huge amounts of work to get them up and running, and all those long hours and late nights hunched in front of the computer on the wrong chair can quickly lead to back problems.

Also, most small businesses rely heavily on a few people. If one or two of these key individuals develops back or neck problems making them unable to work, the effect on the business can be sudden and dramatic. To put it simply, investing in an ergonomic working environment makes complete business sense.

How to create an ergonomic working environment.

A huge array of wellworking products is now available, from brilliantly designed ergonomic furniture (such as the famous Aeron chair), through to sophisticated efficiency software that helps prevent Repetitive Strain Injury and other back and upper limb disorders.

Choosing the right furniture and ergonomic accessories will help keep you and your business healthy, productive and profitable.

Luke Munro is Managing Director of Wellworking, the leading specialists in ergonomic working solutions – from office furniture and accessories to software and consultancy. See **www.wellworking.co.uk** *for more details.*

*UK Health and Safety Executive figures for 2006-7

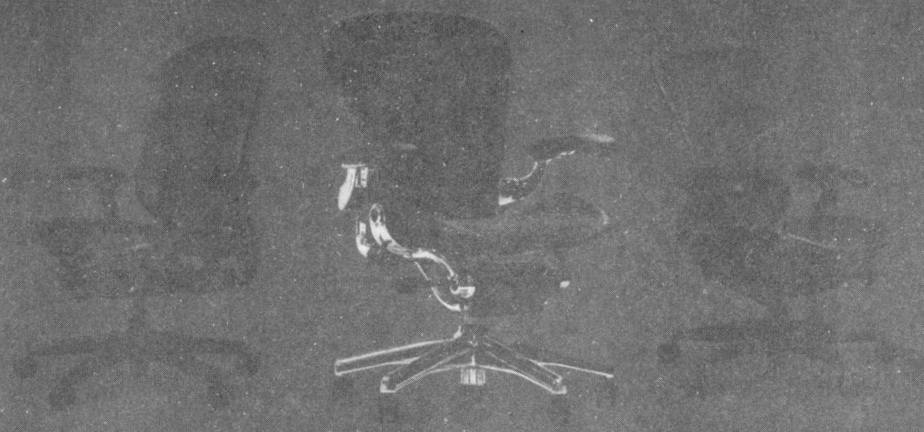

time. Whether you are running or setting up a business, getting a first taste of responsibility for accounts or taking a business course, the first steps towards an understanding of finance are the most difficult. The consequences of failing to understand business finance are not the same for everyone. A student simply fails an exam, while a businessperson all too often loses his or her business and the executive gets fired; competition is generally greater today, and hence the margin for mistakes smaller.

The book is divided into four parts, the first of which begins by explaining what financial data need to be collected and how, in order to be able to keep track of business performance. This bookkeeping process is an essential prerequisite for every type of business, and without it nothing of much value can be established. Bookkeeping itself is hardly a new concept. Luca Pacioli wrote what was in essence the world's first accounting book 500 years ago to help Venetian merchants keep tabs on their ventures. (The 'book' was one of five sections in Pacioli's mathematics book entitled *Everything about Arithmetic, Geometry and Proportions*.) Then there is an introduction to the key financial reports – the cash flow statement, profit-and-loss account and balance sheet; all too often, those trying to get to grips with the problems of poor profits and a negative cash flow miss out these vital building blocks.

The second part builds on this foundation, to show how the raw data can be understood and used to control and direct a business successfully. If you can imagine trying to drive a car without any instruments at all, you will have some impression of how unsatisfactory it would be to run a business without financial controls.

Part 3, 'Figuring out the future', covers the field of budgeting and business planning. Most new ventures cannot get off the ground without a sound business plan, and existing businesses cannot grow without one. A chapter within this section is devoted exclusively to the important task of writing up and presenting a business plan. As this is the 'ticket of entry' to capital, it is important for the business plan to look right.

The final part of the book, 'Dealing with regulatory authorities', covers the vexing and ever-changing area of taxation, the impact of legal structure on accounting, and the responsibilities of directors in matters of finance. Further pressure for an awareness of financial matters has been applied by the Insolvency Act and wrongful trading legislation, which make it an offence for directors to continue trading once they know – or should know – that their business is in trouble. The problem is made more complex by the fast-changing nature of the financial reporting standards that have been adopted in an effort to make accounts more transparent and limit the opportunity for another Enron or Independent Insurance slipping through the net.

I would like to record my appreciation of those 'students' who helped me to focus on key financial issues and sharpen up my thinking generally. In particular the MBA classes at Cranfield School of Management, Suffolk University, Boston, and EM LYON Grande Ecole, the Graduate Enterprise Programme at Stirling University and the Business Growth Programme also at Cranfield. Despite such illustrious assistance any omissions and errors are all my own work!

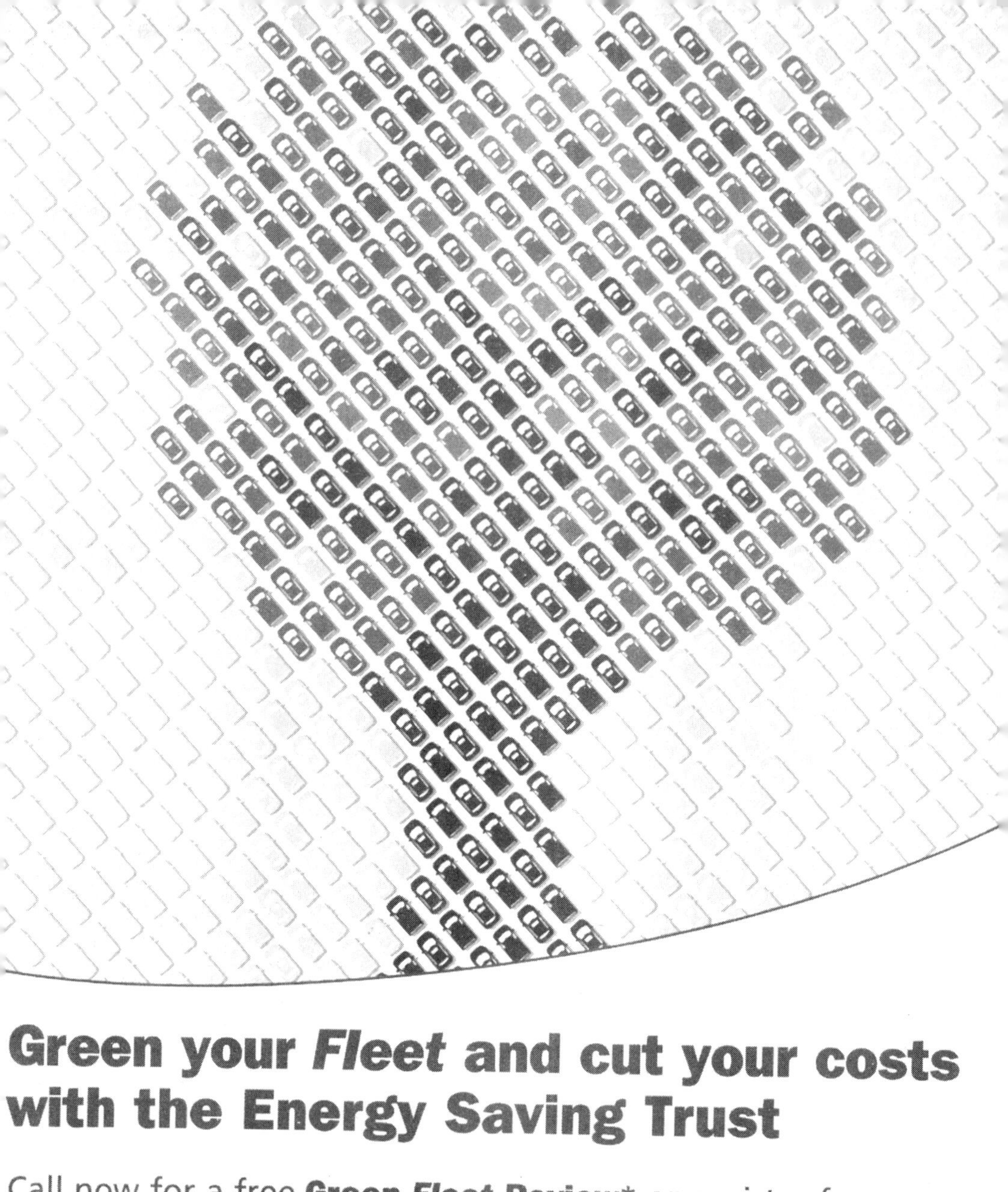

Looking to save money and cut fleet carbon emissions?

The Energy Saving Trust is a not for profit organisation that was set up to help reduce UK carbon emissions, and is part funded by the Department for Transport. Since 2001, we have provided free expert transport advice to hundreds of organisations in England, helping them to significantly cut fuel and transport costs, reduce their carbon footprint, and improve their social and environmental reputation.

Even if you've just started to think about the whole idea of running a greener fleet and how to approach the task, our consultants can help you get a real head start. For organisations that run a fleet of less than 50 vehicles we can provide;

- Telephone advice specifically tailored to your transport needs
- Timely and topical transport advice via our monthly e-bulletin service

We offer advice on all aspects of fleet management including grey fleet (privately owned vehicles for business use), vehicle and fuel choice, mileage reimbursement, mileage reduction strategies, smarter driving and driver education.

For fleets with 50 vehicles or more we offer a free Green Fleet Review, which gives you individual, independent and practical advice on all aspects of your fleet from an environmental perspective. You can also receive formal recognition for your improvements and support for ISO 14001 through our accreditation programme Motorvate.

So whether your fleet challenge is to review your existing fleet policy, reduce transport costs, improve journey planning or become carbon neutral we can help you run a fleet that is greener, leaner and much cleaner than it is today.

To find out more call **0845 602 1425** or visit **www.est.org.uk/transport** to register for our monthly email updates.

There are no costs and no catches – just expert advice tailored to your needs.

1

Assembling financial data

Data processing system

The majority of large international companies now use a business data processing system generically known as 'Enterprise Resource Planning' – ERP. This term is used as the data representing the economic 'resources' of an enterprise are managed and controlled within the same integrated data processing system. Thus, the data and processes supporting the accounting ledgers, stock control, purchase order processing, sales order processing and production order processing are all held and performed within the same integrated software package.

This integrated approach results in accounting staff doing reduced levels of original data entry work, as the majority of ledger postings are automatically created when individual documents are posted by staff in originating departments. Only supplier invoices and cash payments/receipts are handled directly by accounting staff. The time saved by this approach allows accounting staff to perform more investigatory tasks, or even to be reduced in number, thereby reducing costs.

Integrated ERP software systems have now filtered down to small and mid-tier enterprises that can purchase ERP systems for an affordable price, under £10,000 (at time of writing). The advantages of using an ERP system can be summarised as:

- no integration between software systems, reducing complexity
- no reconciliations between systems, reducing running costs
- master data is centrally held, so avoiding duplication and inconsistency
- data flows immediately across all areas, improving monitoring/control
- data is entered once at beginning of process and used many times
- everyone uses the same source data, eliminating inconsistancy
- instant data access enables 'networked economy'
- provides focus on one software supplier for support and maintenance.

Acceptum Business Software is an ERP system for small and mid-tier enterprises providing modules covering:

- accounting ledgers and financial reporting
- sales order processing
- purchase order processing
- production order processing
- stock control
- fixed assets
- development framework for system customisation
- budgeting and forecasting
- project costing
- contact management
- KPI dashboard and scorecard
- time and billing

Acceptum has been built using a unified ledger approach. That is, all accounts are held directly in the General Ledger, be they customers, suppliers, products, or typical expense and balance sheet accounts. Why have we done this? Because, it eliminates the need for internal sub-system reconciliations and it greatly increases the reporting ability of the system. Both, being major advantages to the user.

With Acceptum's unified ledger system, plus its flexible data reporting and drilldown facilities, management has an excellent tool for reviewing data and pin pointing those pertinent records within the mass of normal data.

Web site support

Enterprises with web sites can use Acceptum Business Software for their back office support function, whether the web site is hosted or in-house. Enabling web orders to be completed by standard business processes. Data can be transmitted from the web site via File Transfer Protocol (FTP), e-mail in XML format, or basic file imports. Data can also be exported from Acceptum for the web site to use. File formats available are – Microsoft Excel, CSV, XML, etc. So whether you are taking orders or just storing visitor contact details, Acceptum can help an enterprise to manage and control all its data.

Why Acceptum

Acceptum Business Software supports the processing requirements of an enterprise. Being an organisation that understands the needs of small/mid-tier enterprises', Acceptum is prepared to go that extra mile to achieve a client's data processing goals and provide that vital element - system support. You get a business partner, not just software!

1

Keeping the books

While bad luck plays a part in some business failures, a lack of reliable financial information plays a part in most. All that needs to be done is for the information on income and expenditure to be recorded and organised so that the financial picture becomes clear. The way financial information is recorded is known as 'bookkeeping'.

But it is not just the owner of a company who needs these financial facts. Bankers, shareholders and tax inspectors will be unsympathetic audiences to anyone without well-documented facts to back them up. Keeping even the simplest of records – perhaps as little as writing down the source of a deposit on a slip or in your chequebook and recording the event in a book or ledger – will make your relations with tax inspectors and bankers go much more smoothly.

If you just pile your bills, receipts and cheque stubs into an old shoebox and take it to an accountant at the end of the year (or when you run out of cash), it will cost a lot more to get your accounts done than if you had kept good records in the first place. In addition, you will have had a stressful period of being unsure of how well or badly you are doing.

The accounts you have to keep

There are no rules about the format to be used for a bookkeeping system. Records can be on paper, in ledgers or on a computer. You must, however, be able to show where all your business income came from and who you have paid and for what services. If you are registered for VAT (see below) you will also need to keep a record of the VAT element of each invoice and bill and produce a summary for each accounting period covered by your VAT returns.

Starting simple

If you are doing books by hand and don't have a lot of transactions, the single-entry method is the easiest acceptable way to go. This involves writing down each transaction in your records once, preferably on a ledger sheet. Receipts and payments should be kept and summarised daily, weekly or monthly, in accordance with the needs of the business. At the end of the year, the 12 monthly summaries are totalled up – you are ready for tax time.

Table 1.1 A simple cash-book system

Receipts				**Payments**			
Date	**Name**	**Details**	**Amount £**	**Date**	**Name**	**Details**	**Amount £**
1 June	Balance	Brought forward	450.55	4 June	Gibbs	Stock purchase	310.00
4 June	Anderson	Sales	175.00	8 June	Gibbs	Stock purchase	130.00
6 June	Brown	Sales	45.00	12 June	ABC Telecoms	Telephone charges	55.23
14 June	Smith & Co	Refund on returned stock	137.34	18 June	Colt Rentals	Vehicle hire	87.26
17 June	Jenkins	Sales	190.25	22 June	VV Mobiles	Mobile phone	53.24
20 June	Hollis	Sales	425.12	27 June	Gibbs	Stock purchase	36.28
23 June	Jenkins	Sales	56.89				
							672.01
				30 June	Balance	Carried down	**808.14**
			1,480.15				**1,480.15**
1 July	Balance	Brought down	**808.14**				

This simple record system is known as a 'cash book' – an example is given in Table 1.1.

In the left-hand four columns, the month's expenses are entered as they occur, together with some basic details and the amount. At the head of the first column is the amount of cash brought forward from the preceding month.

On the right, expenses are listed in the same way. The total of receipts for the month is £1,480.15 and that for expenses is £672.01. The difference between these two figures is the amount of cash now in the business. As the business shown in Table 1.1 has brought in more cash than it has spent, the figure is higher than the amount brought forward at the beginning of the month. The figure of £808.14 is the amount that is 'brought down' to be 'brought forward' to the next month. The total of the month's payments and the amount 'carried down' are equal to the sum of all the receipts in the left-hand columns.

If there are a reasonably large number of transactions, it would be sensible to extend this simple cash book to include a basic analysis of the figures – this variation is called an 'analysed cash book'. An example of the payments side of an analysed cash book is shown in Table 1.2 (the receipts side is similar, but with different categories). You can see at a glance the receipts and payments,

Table 1.2 Example of an analysed cash book

Receipts				**Analysis**			
Date	**Name**	**Details**	**Amount £**	**Stocks**	**Vehicles**	**Telephone**	**Other**
4 June	Gibbs	Stock purchase	310.00	310.00			
8 June	Gibbs	Stock purchase	130.00	130.00			
12 June	ABC Telecoms	Telephone charges	55.23			55.23	
18 June	Colt Rentals	Vehicle hire	87.26		87.26		
22 June	VV Mobiles	Mobile phone	53.24			53.24	
27 June	Gibbs	Stock purchase	36.28	36.28			
Totals			**672.01**	**476.28**	**87.26**	**108.47**	

both in total and by main category. This breakdown lets you see, for example, how much is being spent on each major area of your business, or who your most important customers are. The payments are the same as in Table 1.1, but now we can see how much we have spent on stock, vehicles and telephone expenses. The sums total both down the amount columns and across the analysis section to arrive at the same amount: £672.01. This is both a useful bit of management information and essential for your tax return.

If you are taking or giving credit, you will need to keep more information than the cash book – whether it is analysed or not. You will need to keep copies of paid and unpaid sales invoices and the same for purchases, as well as your bank statements. The bank statements should then be 'reconciled' to your cash book to tie everything together. For example, the bank statement for the example given in Table 1.1 should show £808.14 in the account at the end of June. Figure 1.1 outlines how this works.

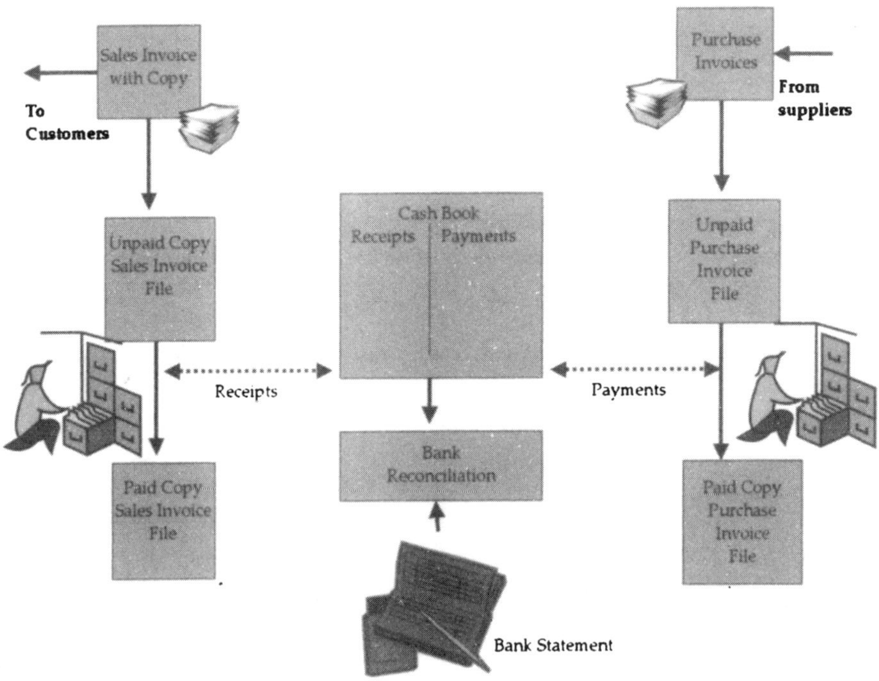

Figure 1.1 A simple system of business records

FREE YOURSELF WITH LIBERTY ACCOUNTS
ONLINE ACCOUNTING, PAYROLL AND STOCK MANAGEMENT
Manage your business finances when & where you want
Collaborate easily with colleagues and advisors
No software installation or upgrade headaches
No backups or disaster recovery worries
Easily file PAYE and VAT returns online directly from Liberty Accounts
"Liberty Accounts is so user friendly I don't eel intimidated..."
Sarah McCaig - MJM Plumbing & Heating Ltd
Your customer service is probably the best 've experienced from anyone - ever..."
Alexander Greene - Greene & Greene Wines
Now I'm doing a job I wouldn't be able to o without Liberty, from wherever I happen o be."
Heidi Hayes - Body Active Chiropractic Clinics
TEL 0845 230 9803
LibertyAccounts.com
online accounting solutions

traditional accounting software, you wont have to buy a package then pay for repeated upgrades, because with Liberty you pay an affordable fixed monthly fee.

As well as fitting in with the way you want to run your business, Liberty can grow with it. 'Ten years ago the only employee was me, but as we've grown we've taken on staff,' says Keith Owen of Interactive Marketing Ltd, and it no longer made financial sense for him to manage his payroll manually. 'My time became too valuable,' says the director, and because Liberty Accounts can handle payroll as well as bookkeeping, it makes all aspects of the businesses finances easier to manage.

'Liberty memorises the details for our regular monthly invoices and produces them automatically,' enthuses Owen, and it's easy to make adjustments. 'It used to take me two solid days to do the payroll for my 55 staff,' he adds, and now it takes three hours, and the PAYE year-end is also much easier. 'Previously it took me two or three weeks, and now it's done in a couple of hours.'

Liberty Accounts can also help you to get more from your bookkeeper or accountant, because the online approach makes it easier to share information with them. 'I've used Liberty for almost a whole financial year, and it has transformed my business accounting,' says Ann Lewis, a leadership and executive coach. 'I have full access to my accounting history,' she adds, 'and because my accountant can also access the system directly the whole process is transparent, and problems are easy to sort out.'

If you want to make your bookkeeping and payroll less complicated contact Alan Wright at Liberty Accounts on ***0845 230 9803***
or visit ***www.libertyaccounts.com***

Building a system

If you operate a partnership, trade as a company or plan to get big, then you will need a double-entry bookkeeping system. This calls for a series of day books, ledgers, a journal, a petty-cash book and a wages book, as well as a number of files for copies of invoices and receipts.

The double-entry system requires two entries for each transaction – this provides built-in checks and balances to ensure accuracy. Each transaction requires an entry as a debit and as a credit. This may sound a little complicated, but you only need to get a general idea.

A double-entry system is more complicated and time-consuming if done by hand, since everything is recorded twice. If done manually, the method requires a formal set of books – journals and ledgers. All transactions are first entered into a journal and then 'posted' (written) on a ledger sheet – the same amount is written down in two different places. Typical ledger accounts include those for titled income, expenses, assets and liabilities (debts).

To give an example, a payment of rent in a double-entry system might result in two separate journal entries – a debit for an expense of, say, £250 and a corresponding credit of £250 – a double entry (see Table 1.3). The debits in a double-entry system must always equal the credits. If they don't, you know there is an error somewhere. So, double entry allows you to balance your books, which you can't do with the single-entry method.

Table 1.3 An example of a double-entry ledger

General Journal of Andrew's Bookshop			
Date	**Description of entry**	**Debit**	**Credit**
10th July	Rent expense	£250.00	
	Cash		£250.00

Paper-based bookkeeping systems

If you expect to have fewer than 50 transactions each month, either buying or selling, then you can simply use analysis paper, either loose or in books that are available from any larger stationer. These are sheets of paper of A3 size, with a dozen or so lined columns already drawn, so you can enter figures and extend your analysis, as shown in Table 1.2. Alternatively you can buy a manual accounting system with a full set of ledgers and books for around £20 from Hingston Publishing Co (www.hingston-publishing.co.uk) or Collins Account Books, available from most larger stationers.

Getting some help

You don't have to do the bookkeeping yourself, though if you do for the first year or so you will get a good insight into how your business works from a financial perspective. There are a number of ways in which you can reduce or even eliminate the more tedious aspects of the task.

Bookkeeping and accounting software

With the cost of a basic computerised bookkeeping and accounting system starting at barely £50, and a reasonable package costing between £200 and £500, it makes good sense to plan to use such a system from the outset. Key advantages include having no more arithmetical errors and speedy preparation of VAT returns, and preparing your accounts at the year end will be a whole lot simpler.

Sourcing accounting and bookkeeping software

There are dozens of perfectly satisfactory basic accounting and bookkeeping software packages on the market. The leading providers are:

- Dosh (www.dosh.co.uk);
- Microsoft Money (www.microsoft.co.uk);
- MYOB (My Own Business) (www.myob.co.uk);
- QuickBooks (www.intuit.co.uk/store/en/quickbooks/index.jsp);
- Sage (www.uk.sage.com);
- Simplex (www.simplex.net);
- TAS (www.tassoftware.co.uk).

Using a bookkeeping service

Two professional associations, the International Association of Book-keepers (IAB) (tel: 01732 458080; www.iab.org.uk) and the Institute of Certified Book-keepers (tel: 0845 060 2345; www.book-keepers.org), offer free matching services to help small businesses find a bookkeeper to suit their particular needs. Expect to pay upwards of £20 an hour for services that can be as basic as simply recording the transactions in your books, through to producing accounts, preparing the VAT return or doing the payroll.

Hiring an accountant

If you plan to trade as a partnership or limited company, are approaching the VAT threshold of around £67,000 annual turnover or look as though you will be making over £20,000 net profit before tax you may be ready to hire an accountant to look after your books.

Finding an accountant

Personal recommendation from someone in your business network is the best starting point to find an accountant. Meet the person and if you think you could work with him or her, take up references as you would with anyone you employ and make sure the person is a qualified member of one of the professional bodies. The Association of Chartered Certified Accountants (www.accaglobal.com > Public interest > Find an accountant) and the Institute of Chartered Accountants (www.icaewfirms.co.uk) have online directories of qualified accountants, which you can search by name, location, the business sector you are in or any specific accountancy skills you are looking for.

2

The cash flow statement

There is a saying in business that profit is vanity and cash flow is sanity. Both are necessary, but in the short term – and often that is all that matters to a new business as it struggles to get a foothold in the shifting sands of trading – cash flow is life or death.

Why cash is king

One of the characteristics that most new or small businesses have in common is a tendency to change their size and shape quickly. In the early months and years customers are few, and each new customer (or particularly big order) can mean a large percentage increase in sales. A large increase in sales in turn means an increase in raw materials and perhaps more wages and other expenses. Generally, these expenses have to be met before your customer pays up, and until the money comes in the business has to find cash to meet its bills. If it cannot find the cash to meet these day-to-day bills, then it becomes 'illiquid' and very often goes bust.

So, paradoxically, while profit is undoubtedly the goal of business, you have to survive to enjoy those profits, and having cash or access to liquid funds is what lets a business live long enough to enjoy the fruits of its labour.

The structure of the cash flow statement

The future is impossible to predict with great accuracy, but it is possible to anticipate likely outcomes and be prepared to deal with events by building in a margin of safety. The starting point for preparing a cash flow statement is to make some assumptions about what you want to achieve and testing those for reasonableness.

Take the situation of High Note, a home-based business being established to sell sheet music, small instruments and CDs to schools and colleges, which will expect trade credit, and members of the public, who will pay cash. The owner plans to invest £10,000 and to borrow £10,000 from a bank on a long-term basis. The business will be run out of a double garage adjoining the owner's home and will require £11,500 for the installation of windows, heat, light, power, storage shelving and a desk and chairs. A further £1,000 will be needed for a computer, software and a printer. That should leave around £7,500 to meet immediate trading expenses such as buying in stock and spending £1,500 on initial advertising. Hopefully customer's payments will start to come in quickly to cover other expenses such as some wages for bookkeeping, administration and fulfilling orders. Sales in the first six months are expected to be £60,000 based on negotiations already in hand, plus some cash sales that always seem to turn up. The rule of thumb in the industry seems to be that stock is marked up by 100 per cent; so £30,000 of bought-in goods sell on for £60,000.

Forecasting cash needs

On the basis of the above assumptions it is possible to make the cash flow forecast set out in Table 2.1. It has been simplified, and some elements such as VAT and tax have been omitted for ease of understanding.

The maths in Table 2.1 is straightforward; the cash receipts from various sources are totalled, as are the payments. Taking one from the other leaves a cash surplus or deficit for the month in question. The bottom row shows the cumulative position. So, for example, while the business had £2,450 cash left at the end of April, taking the cash deficit of £1,500 in May into account, by the end of May only £950 (£2,450 – £1,500) cash remains.

Avoiding overtrading

In the example above the business has insufficient cash, based on the assumptions made. An outsider, a banker perhaps, would look at the figures in August and see that the faster sales grew the greater the cash flow deficit became. We know, using our crystal ball, that the position will improve from September and that if we can only hang on in there for a few more months we should eliminate

Table 2.1 High Note six-month cash flow forecast

Month	Apr	May	June	July	Aug	Sep	Total
Receipts:							
Sales	4,000	5,000	5,000	7,000	12,000	15,000	48,000
Owner's cash	10,000						
Bank loan	10,000						
Total cash in	24,000	5,000	5,000	7,000	12,000	15,000	
Payments:							
Purchases	5,500	2,950	4,220	7,416	9,332	9,690	39,108
Rates, electricity, heat, telephone, internet, etc	1,000	1,000	1,000	1,000	1,000	1,000	
Wages	1,000	1,000	1,000	1,000	1,000	1,000	
Advertising	1,550	1,550	1,550	1,550	1,550	1,550	
Fixtures/fittings	11,500						
Computer, etc	1,000						
Total cash out	21,550	6,500	7,770	10,966	12,882	13,240	
Monthly cash surplus/(deficit)	2,450	(1,500)	(2,770)	(3,966)	(882)	1,760	
Cumulative cash balance	2,450	950	(1,820)	(5,786)	(6,668)	(4,908)	

our cash deficit and perhaps even have a surplus. Had we made the cash flow projection at the outset and raised more money, perhaps by way of an overdraft, spent less on refurbishing our garage, or set a more modest sales goal, hence needing less stock and advertising, we would have had a sound business. The figures indicate a business that is trading beyond its financial resources, a condition known as overtrading and anathema to bankers the world over.

Estimating start-up cash requirements

The example above takes the cash flow projection out six months. You should project your cash needs forward for between 12 and 18 months. Make a number of projections using differing assumptions, for example seeing what will happen if you get fewer orders, people take longer to buy or adapting your office costs more. Finally, when you arrive at a projection you have confidence in and you believe you can justify the cash needed, build that figure into the financing needs section of your business plan.

If that projection calls for more money than you are prepared to invest or raise from outside don't just steam ahead and hope for the best. The result could well mean that the bank pulls the plug on you when you are within sight of the winning post. There is a useful spreadsheet that will prompt you through the most common costs on the Startups website (www.startups.co.uk > Business planning > Startup costs).

Cash flow spreadsheet tools

You can do a number of 'what if' projections to fine-tune your cash flow projections using a spreadsheet. Business Link (www.businesslink.gov.uk/Finance_files/Cash_Flow_Projection_Worksheet.xls) has a cash flow spreadsheet that you can copy and paste into an Excel file on your computer; Small Business Advice Service (www.smallbusinessadvice.org.uk > Free downloads > Download cashflow forecast) has a free spreadsheet you can download online.

3

The profit-and-loss account

You may by now be concerned about the financial situation at High Note as revealed in the preceding chapter. After all the business has sold £60,000 worth of goods that it only paid £30,000 for, so it has a substantial profit margin to play with. Whilst £39,108 has been paid to suppliers, only £30,000 of goods at cost have been sold, meaning that £9,108 worth of instruments, sheet music and CDs are still in our stock. A similar situation exists with sales. We have billed for £60,000 but only been paid for £48,000; the balance is owed by debtors. The bald figure at the end of the cash flow projection showing High Note to be in the red to the tune of £4,908 seems to be missing some important facts.

The difference between profit and cash

Cash is immediate and takes account of nothing else. Profit, however, is a measurement of economic activity that considers other factors that can be assigned a value or cost. The accounting principle that governs profit is known as the 'matching principle', which means that income and expenditure are matched to the time period in which they occur.

So for High Note the profit-and-loss account for the first six months would be as shown in Table 3.1.

Structuring the profit-and-loss account

This account is set out in more detail for a business in order to make it more useful when it comes to understanding how a business is performing. For

Table 3.1 Profit-and-loss account for High Note for the six months April–September

	£	£
Sales		60,000
Less cost of goods to be sold		30,000
Gross profit		30,000
Less expenses:		
Rates, electricity, heat, telephone, internet, etc	6,000	
Wages	6,000	
Advertising	9,300	
Total expenses		21,300
Profit before tax, interest and depreciation charges		8,700

example, though the profit shown in our worked example is £8,700, in fact it would be rather lower. As money has been borrowed to finance cash flow there would be interest due, as there would be on the longer-term loan of £10,000.

In practice we have four levels of profit:

- Gross profit is the profit left after all costs related to making what you sell are deducted from income.
- Operating profit is what's left after you take the operating expenses away from the gross profit.
- Profit before tax is what is left after deducting any financing costs.
- Profit after tax is what is left for the owners to spend or reinvest in the business.

For High Note this could look much as set out in Table 3.2 (page 24).

A more comprehensive structure

Once a business has been trading for a few years it will have taken on a wide range of new commitments. For example, as well as the owner's money, there may be a long-term loan to be serviced (interest and capital repayments), or parts of the workshop or offices may be sublet. Like any accounting report, the profit-and-loss account should be prepared in the best form for the user, bearing in mind the requirements of the regulatory authorities (see Part 4). The elements to be included are:

RBS
The Royal Bank of Scotland

Contact

RBS Invoice Finance
Smith House
Elmwood Avenue
Feltham
Middlesex
TW13 7QD

Telephone:
0800 711 911*
*Lines are open 9.00am – 17.00pm Monday to Friday

Email:
invoicefinance@rbs.co.uk

Web:
www.rbsif.co.uk

Association Memberships

Asset Based Finance Association

RBS Invoice Finance

RBS Invoice Finance is one of the UK's leading Invoice Finance providers and part of The Royal Bank of Scotland Group.

Waiting up to 90 days or more for invoices to be settled can create real cash flow issues and can impact on your growth potential. With RBS Invoice Finance, you could release up to 90% of the value of your invoices immediately, with the rest to follow when they are settled.*

RBS Invoice Finance can be more than a cash flow solution, we have helped clients to raise funds for MBOs and MBIs.

Call us today to find out how we can help your business.

*Less our charges.

Services and Products

Factoring

Credit Management

Invoice Discounting

Bad Debt Protection

Export/Import service with multi-currency capability

MBOs/MBIs

Financing For Growth

Steve Bentley, Director Business Development at RBS Invoice Finance comments

Planning for growth inevitably sees companies reaching for their financial planners, and consulting advisors on their various funding options. With loans or overdrafts arranged, it would be easy to presume that the headache was over, but for many company directors it may have only just begun.

For example, many businesses seem to accept that late payment is an inevitable part of commercial life - even though they lose on average 17 days a year chasing overdue invoices and are owed some £18.6billion at any one time according to BACS.

A successful growing business will often be a business selling more to more customers, growing turnover – but that will also increase the amount of money owed back from unpaid invoices, and therefore increasing the working capital cashflow requirement of the business – the more successful they become.

Efficient cash flow solutions are the order of the day for a business to survive and grow effectively. What many business people need is not only financial help for the long-term, but also a helping hand to make cash available on a day-to-day basis to pay staff and suppliers.

Cash represents the life-blood of the business. At the very least a firm requires access to sufficient cash balances to meet its day-to-day overheads, and to act as a buffer in the event of delayed payments and bad debts. Some firms do not anticipate all their expenses and discover, when it is often too late, that their business is at risk. One of the most important considerations for firms is to put cash flow first, profit second and turnover last. A survey conducted by the Forum of Private Business recorded that just £20,000 of overdue invoices could push a third of small and medium-sized firms out of business and three in four admit that late payment is a "considerable threat" to the viability of their business.

So what steps should businesses be looking to take to protect their future? Invoice finance works on the basic principle that the invoice finance

1. sales (and any other revenues from operations);
2. cost of sales (or cost of goods sold);
3. gross profit – the difference between sales and cost of sales;
4. operating expenses – selling, administration, depreciation and other general costs;
5. operating profit – the difference between gross profit and operating expenses;
6. non-operating revenues – other revenues, including interest, rent, etc;
7. non-operating expenses – financial costs and other expenses not directly related to the running of the business;
8. profit before income tax;
9. provision for income tax;
10. net income (or profit or loss).

Table 3.2 High Note extended profit-and-loss account

	£
Sales	60,000
Less the cost of goods to be sold	30,000
Gross profit	30,000
Less operating expenses	21,300
Operating profit	8,700
Less interest on bank loan and overdraft	600
Profit before tax	8,100
Less tax	1,377
Profit after tax	6,723

Dealing with debtors and creditors

While the cash flow statement deals with the reality of cash movements, the profit-and-loss account sets out to 'match' income and expenditure to the time period when the event took place. In order to make such matches a number of rules and conventions are followed.

Recognizing income

A particularly prudent sales manager once said that an order was not an order until the customer's cheque had cleared, the customer had consumed the product and had not died as a result, and, finally, he or she had shown every indication of wanting to buy again. Most of us know quite different salespeople who can 'anticipate' the most unlikely volume of sales. In accounting, income is usually recognized as having been earned when the goods (or services) are dispatched and the invoice sent out. This has nothing to do with when an order is received, how firm an order is or how likely a customer is to pay up promptly.

It is also possible that some of the products dispatched may be returned at some later date – perhaps for quality reasons. This means that income, and consequently profit, can be brought into the business in one period and have to be removed later on. Obviously, if these returns can be estimated accurately, then an adjustment can be made to income at the time. So the 'sales income' figure that is seen at the top of a profit and loss account is the value of the goods dispatched (or services executed) and invoiced to customers in the period in question.

Handling creditors

Creditors – people you owe money to – are dealt with in the profit-and-loss account in the same way as debtors, those who owe you money. If the item you have purchased has been used or consumed in the products or services you have sold, it needs to be taken into the expense element of the profit-and-loss account. If, for example, the purchase has not been used, as is the case with raw materials and other consumables used in production, then anything bought and not used will show up in the balance sheet (see Chapter 4) as finished goods, work in progress or raw materials in the current asset category.

Invisible accruals

Accruing is a general name for the form of accounting where a figure is put in before the cash event has occurred. There is one particular type of accrual that calls for greater judgement and that is when the item in question has not yet shown up in the paperwork. Usually you can rely on people to send in their bills on time, and often suppliers will deliver only after you have paid up. But consider how you should handle a quarterly telephone bill that comes in after you have completed the profit-and-loss account for the year, but includes a month of that year. You could ignore it in that year's accounts, as after all you have no documentary evidence that it exists: doing that would overstate profits for the period concerned and understate them for the following period. The correct procedure is to accrue a sum of expense that is your best estimate of what the actual telephone expense was for that month and put that figure into that year, leaving the remaining sum for the following period.

Handling depreciation

A further important factor is how to treat capital expenditure on fixed assets over time. If we take as expense the whole sum for a major item of equipment that has a working life of several years into just the year in which it has been bought, our figures will be unfairly distorted. Such fixed assets are usually depreciated over their working life rather than taken as one hit on the profit-and-loss account. There are accounting rules on the appropriate period to depreciate different assets over, usually somewhere between three and 20 years.

If we believe a computer costing £1,000 has a useful life of four years and the rules allow it, we take £250 a year of cost, by way of depreciation, as an expense item in the profit-and-loss account for the year in question. Depreciation, though vital for your management accounts, is not an allowable expense for tax purposes. The tax authorities allow a 'writing down' allowance, say of 25 per cent, of the cost of an asset each year, which can be set as an expense for tax purposes. There are periods when the government of the day wants to stimulate businesses to invest, say in computers, and they will boost the writing down allowance accordingly. This figure will almost certainly not correspond to your estimate of depreciation, so you need a profit for tax purposes and a profit for management purposes.

Depreciation is entered as a figure in the expenses of the profit-and-loss account, as well as being shown cumulatively in the balance sheet.

Cost of goods sold

Now you may consider that everything you have spent in the business has gone into 'making' the product, but to calculate the cost of goods sold, only costs strictly concerned with making are considered. These will include the cost of all materials and the cost of manufacturing labour.

After blowing up the cost of goods sold section, a profit-and-loss account could look like Table 3.3. This is not a complete list of items we would find in the cost of goods sold section of a manufacturer's profit-and-loss account. For

Table 3.3 Example of a profit-and-loss account for a small manufacturing company including cost of goods sold

Hardcourt Ltd
Profit-and-loss account for the year ended 31 December

	£	£	£
Sales			100,000
Manufacturing costs			
Raw materials opening stock	30,000		
Purchases in period	25,000		
	55,000		
Less Raw materials closing stock	15,500		
Cost of materials used		39,500	
Direct labour cost		18,000	
Manufacturing overhead cost			
Indirect labour	4,000		
Workshop heat, light and power	3,500		
Total manufacturing costs		7,500	
Cost of goods sold			65,000
Gross profit			35,000

example, work in progress, plant depreciation, etc have been ignored to keep the example clear enough for the principle to be established.

Profit and loss for a service business

All the basic principles and practices of the manufacturing business apply to a service or professional business. The main area of difference will be in the calculation of gross profit. For example, a consultancy organisation's profit-and-loss account could look like Table 3.4.

Or a travel agency's profit-and-loss account might look like Table 3.5.

Table 3.4 Example of a consultancy organisation's profit-and-loss account

Thames Consultants		
	£	£
Sales	65,000	
Fees paid to consultants	30,000	
Profit before expenses (gross profit)		35,000
Expenses, etc (as for any other business)	...	

Table 3.5 Example of a travel agency's profit-and-loss account

Sunburn Travel	
	£
Sales	200,000
Payments to carriers	130,000
Net commission income (gross profit)	70,000
Expenses, etc (as for any other business)	...

Table 3.6 Example of a profit-and-loss account showing sales revenue of different products

Domestic Furniture Ltd		
Sales:	£	£
Tables	50,000	
Chairs	20,000	
Repairs, etc	10,000	
		80,000
Cost of goods sold		50,000
Gross profit		30,000
Less expenses (as for any other business)		...

Sales analysis

It may be useful to show the sales revenue by each major product group, as in Table 3.6, and by home and export sales, if appropriate. It would be even more useful to show the gross margin by major product.

Profit-and-loss spreadsheet tool

There is an online spreadsheet at SCORE's website (www.score.org > Business tools > Template gallery > Profit and loss). Download it in Excel format and you have a profit-and-loss account with 30 lines of expenses, the headings of which you can change or delete to meet your particular needs.

4

The balance sheet

There is a much told Irish story of the driver lost on his travels between Dublin and Cork. He stopped to ask the way of a passing farmer, who replied, 'If I were going to Cork I wouldn't start from here'.

For people in business this is an all too pertinent answer. We nearly always need a good idea of where we are now if we are to have any chance of reaching our goal. But either through pressures of more immediate tasks, or the nagging feeling that we will not like the answers, sizing up the financial situation is a job relegated to the bottom of the pile.

Even in our private lives it is helpful to 'strike a balance' when important financial issues are at stake. Questions such as should we move house, buy a boat, a new car, or take a holiday involve us in an informal sizing up of the situation before making a decision.

A personal experience

This example looks at the finances of Terry Brown. She has become a little confused by the complexity of her financial affairs and has decided to get things sorted out. In short, she wants to know where she is.

If you were to summarise your present financial position it would contain, at least, some elements of the example given in Table 4.1.

This information tells us something of Terry's circumstances, but until we organise the information we cannot really understand her true financial position.

Terry believes that in money matters things divide neatly into two: things you have and things you owe, with the latter usually exceeding the former. So,

Table 4.1 Example summary of financial position

Terry Brown – Financial position today (28 March) 1

	£
Cash	50
House	50,000
Mortgage	45,000
Money owed by sister (Jackie)	135
Overdraft	100
Car (Citroën 2CV)	1,000
Credit cards	50
Jewellery and paintings	350
Hire purchase (on various goods)	500
Furniture	500

Table 4.2 Example summary of financial position showing assets, liabilities and claims

Terry Brown – Financial position today (28 March) 2

Liabilities and claims (Where I got the money from)	£	Assets (What I have done with the money)	£
Overdraft	100	Cash	50
Mortgage	45,000	House	50,000
Hire purchase	500	Car	1,000
Credit cards	50	Jewellery and paintings	350
Total claims by other people	45,650	Money owed by sister	135
My capital	6,385	Furniture	500
Total of my and other people's money	52,035	My assets	52,035

using this concept and slightly different words, we could show the same information in the manner shown in Table 4.2. On the right-hand side we have made a list of Terry's *assets*: what she has done with the money she has had. On the left is listed where she got the money from to pay for these assets: the *liabilities and claims* against her.

You may have got a little lost towards the bottom of the left-hand column. This is simply because we have to try and show the complete picture of Terry's financial affairs. She has acquired £52,035 worth of assets and must have provided an identical sum from one source or another. We can find only £45,650 owed to other people. The only reasonable assumption is that Terry herself must have put in the balance over the past years. In other words, she has put her past salary or wages towards buying the assets.

Now while Terry might be happy with the help we have given her so far, it is unlikely she will be completely satisfied. Like the rest of us, she probably considers events as long- or short-term in nature. Even though we have shown a fairly dazzling picture of £50,000+ of assets, she knows she is short of cash for day-to-day living. So once again we could restructure the information on her financial position to give a clearer picture (Table 4.3).

Table 4.3 Example summary of financial position showing long- and short-term assets, liabilities and claims

Terry Brown – Financial position today (28 March) 3

Liabilities (long term) (Where I got the money from)	£	Fixed assets (long term) (What I have done with the money)	£
Mortgage	45,000	House	50,000
Hire purchase	500	Car	1,000
		Furniture	500
My capital	6,385	Jewellery and paintings	350
	51,885		51,850
Current liabilities (short term)		Current assets (short term)	
Overdraft	100	Money owed by sister	135
Credit cards	50	Cash	50
	150		185
Total liabilities	52,035	Total assets	52,035

For example, we can now see that her short-term financial position is dominated by the money her sister owes her. If that is safe, then all current liabilities can be met. If it is not safe, and that money is unlikely to be repaid quickly, the position is not too good. There is an accounting convention according to which 'current' liabilities are those that we will have to pay within a year. Similarly, 'current' assets will turn into cash within a year.

We are getting very close to having a *balance sheet* of Terry's financial position. One further adjustment will reveal all. It is vital that both the long- and short-term financial positions are readily visible to the examiner. Terry's day-to-day assets and liabilities need to be clearly highlighted. What we are looking for is the net position: how much she currently owes, subtracted from how much she has.

By redrafting the financial position, we shall see the whole picture more clearly (Table 4.4): £51,850 is tied up in *fixed assets* and £35 is tied up in *net current assets*. All these have been *financed by* £6,385 of Terry's capital and £45,500 which has been provided by a mortgage and a hire purchase company.

The public picture

Terry Brown found it useful to have a clear picture of her current financial position. A business will find such a picture essential. While most people are responsible only to themselves and their families, businesses have a wider audience. Partners, bankers, shareholders, financial institutions, and HM Revenue & Customs are only a few of the possible interested parties, apart from the owners' and managers' interest in the financial situation, which is taken for granted.

All these interested parties keep track of a business's financial performance by having a series of reports, or statements, prepared. In effect a business acts as a steward of other people's money and it is to give account of this stewardship that these financial records are prepared. While these 'figure' statements provide usual evidence, it is as well to remember that the evidence is only partial: nothing in Terry's balance sheet has told us that she is female, 27 years old and currently sporting a carrot-red head of hair.

Another important limitation on these financial statements is the reliability of the figures themselves. The cash-in-hand figure is probably dead right, but can the same be said of the furniture values? Accountants have their own rules on how these figures are to be arrived at, but they do not pretend to anything better than an approximation. Every measuring device has inherent inaccuracies, and financial controls are no exception.

Table 4.4 Example balance sheet

Terry Brown – Balance sheet 28 March

Fixed assets		£
House		50,000
Car		1,000
Furniture		500
Jewellery and paintings		350
		51,850
Current assets		
Money owed by sister		135
Cash		50
		185
Less *Current liabilities*		
Overdraft		100
Credit cards		50
		150
So, Net current assets		35
Total assets, *less* Current liabilities		51,885
Financed by		
My capital		6,385
Mortgage	45,000	
Hire purchase	500	45,500
Total		51,885

Not all the information that we need to prepare a financial statement is always readily on hand. For example, Terry has not had a statement on her credit card account since February (the preceding month), so despite the incomplete data, she has made an educated guess at the current position.

With these questions of reliability in mind, let us now look at how a business monitors and controls its financial position.

The structure of the business balance sheet

You might have noticed that we stopped calling Terry's statement a financial position, and called it a balance sheet in the last example. This is one of the principal business control reports. It is designed to show what assets the business is using at a particular time, and where it got the money to finance those assets. The balance sheet is usually a statement of the present position, but, of course, once a business has been in existence for some time there will be historical balance sheets. These can be used to compare performance in one year (period) with another. This use of the balance sheet will be examined in the chapters on financial control.

It is also possible to prepare a projected balance sheet to show what the future financial picture might look like, given certain assumptions. We shall look at this aspect in more detail in the chapters on planning and budgeting.

You will notice a number of differences between the business balance sheet in Table 4.5 and the personal one we looked at before. But there are also many basic similarities.

First, you will notice the date at the top. This is essential, as the balance sheet is a picture of the business at a particular moment in time. The picture could look quite different tomorrow.

You can also see that some different terms are used for the account categories. Before looking at the main elements of this balance sheet it will be useful to describe the key terms, assets and liabilities.

A balance sheet for a small business might look something like Table 4.5.

Assets

Accountants describe assets as 'valuable resources, owned by a business, which were accrued at a measurable money cost'. You can see that there are three key points in the definition:

1. To be valuable the resource must be cash, or of some use in generating current or future profits. For example, a debtor (someone who owes a business money for goods or services provided) usually pays up. When he or she does, the debtor becomes cash and so meets this test. If there is no hope of getting payment then you can hardly view the sum as an asset.

Table 4.5 High Note balance sheet at 30 September

	£	£
Assets		
Fixed assets:		
Garage conversion, etc	11,500	
Computer	1,000	
Total fixed assets		12,500
Working capital:		
Current assets:		
Stock	9,108	
Debtors	12,000	
Cash	0	
	21,108	
Less: Current liabilities:		
Overdraft	4,908	
Creditors	0	
	4,908	
Working capital (CA – CL)		16,200
Total assets		28,700
Liabilities		
Owner's capital introduced	10,000	
Long-term loan	10,000	
Profit retained (from P&L account)	8,700	
Total liabilities		28,700

2. Ownership, in its legal sense, can be seen as different from possession or control. The accounting use of the word is similar but not identical. In a business, possession and control are not enough to make a resource an asset. For example, a leased machine may be possessed and controlled by a business but be owned by the leasing company. So not only is it not an asset, it is a regular expense. (More about expenses in the next chapter.)
3. Most business resources are bought for a 'measurable money cost'. Often this test is all too painfully obvious. If you pay cash for something, or promise to pay at a later date, it is clearly an asset. If the resource was

manufactured by the business, then money was paid in wages, materials, etc during that process. There may be problems in deciding exactly what money figure to put down, but there is no problem in seeing that money has been spent.

The asset 'goodwill' is one important grey area of particular interest to those buying or selling a small business.

Ranking of assets

There is a useful convention that recommends listing assets in the balance sheet in their order of permanence, that is, starting out with the most difficult to turn into cash and working down to cash itself. This structure is very practical when you are looking at someone else's balance sheet, or comparing balance sheets. It can also help you to recognise obvious information gaps quickly.

Liabilities

These are the claims by people outside the business. In our examples only creditors are shown, but they could include such items as: tax; accruals; deferred income; overdrafts, etc. The 'financed by' section of our example balance sheet is considered in part as liabilities.

Current

This is the term used with both assets and liabilities to show that they will be converted into cash, or have a short life (under one year).

Now let's go through the main elements of the balance sheet.

Net assets employed

This is the 'What have we done with the money?' section. A business can only do three things with funds:

1. It can buy *fixed assets*, such as premises, machinery and motor cars. These are assets that the business intends to keep over the longer term. They will be used to help make profits, but will not physically vanish in the short term (unless sold and replaced, like motor cars, for example).

2. Money can be tied up in *working capital*, that is, 'things' immediately involved in the business's products (or services) that will vanish in the short term. Stocks get sold and are replaced; debtors pay up, and creditors are paid; and cash circulates. Working capital is calculated by subtracting the current liabilities from the current assets. This is the net sum of money that a business has to find to finance the working capital. In the balance sheet this is called the *net current assets*, but on most other occasions the term working capital is used.
3. Finally, a business can put money aside over the longer term, perhaps in local government bonds or as an investment in someone else's business venture. In the latter case this could be a prelude to takeover. In the former it could be a cash reserve for future capital investment. The account category is called *investments*. It is not shown in this example as it is a fairly rare phenomenon in new or small businesses, which are usually cash hungry rather than rich.

Financed by

This section of the balance sheet shows where the money came from. It usually has at least three subheadings, although larger companies can have many more.

1. The *owner's capital introduced* shows the money put into the business by the proprietor. If this was the balance sheet of a limited company it would be called share capital. There could then follow a list of different types of share, for example, preference and ordinary shares.
2. The second source of funds is the *profits* ploughed back into the business to help it grow. In this example £8,700 was retained from profit made in previous periods. Another term in common use is *reserves*, which conjures up pictures of sums of cash stored away for a rainy day. It is important to remember that this is not necessarily so. The only cash in a business is that shown under that heading in the current assets. The reserves, like all the other funds, are used to finance a business and are already tied up elsewhere in the business in such items as fixed assets, stock and debtors.
3. The final source of money to finance a business is long-term *loans* from outside parties. These loans could be in the form of debentures, a mortgage, hire purchase agreements or long-term loans from a bank. The common features of all such loans are that businesses have to pay interest on the money, and eventually repay the capital whether or not the

business is successful. Conversely, if the business is a spectacular success the lenders, unlike the shareholders, will not share in the extra profits.

The ground rules, concepts and conventions

Accounting is certainly not an exact science. Even the most enthusiastic member of the profession would not make that claim. As we have already seen, there is considerable scope for interpretation and educated guesswork. Obviously, if this were to go on unbridled no one inside or outside the business would place any reliance on the figures, so certain ground rules have been laid down by the profession to help get a level of consistency into accounting information.

1. *Money measurement.* In accounting, a record is kept only of the facts that can be expressed in money terms. For example, the state of the managing director's health and the news that your main competitor is opening up right opposite in a more attractive outlet are important business facts. No accounting record of them is made, however, and they do not show up on the balance sheet, simply because no objective monetary value can be assigned to these facts.

   Expressing business facts in money terms has the great advantage of providing a common denominator. Just imagine trying to add computers and motor cars, together with a 4,000 square foot workshop, and then arriving at a total. You need a common term to be able to carry out the basic arithmetical functions, and to compare one set of accounts with another.

   There is one great danger with expressing things in money terms. It suggests that all the pounds are identical. This is not always so. Pounds currently shown as cash in a balance sheet are not exactly the same, for example, as debtors' pounds that may not be turned into cash for many months. The ways of examining this changing value of money over time are looked at in Chapter 10.
2. *Business entity.* The accounts are kept for the business itself, rather than for the owner(s), workers, or anyone else associated with the firm. If an owner puts a short-term cash injection into his business, it will appear as a loan under current liabilities in the business account. In his personal

account it will appear as an asset – money someone else owes him. So depending on which point of view you take, the same sum of money can be an asset or a liability. And as in this example the owner and the business are substantially the same person, the possibilities of confusion are considerable. This source of possible confusion must be cleared up and the business entity concept does just that.

The concept states that assets and liabilities are always defined from the business's viewpoint. Once again it is this idea of stewardship that forces us to see the business as an entity separate from *all* outside parties.

3. *Cost concept.* Assets are usually entered into the accounts at cost. For a variety of reasons, the real 'worth' of an asset will probably change over time.

   The worth, or value, of an asset is a subjective estimate which no two people are likely to agree on. This is made even more complex, and artificial, because the assets themselves are usually not for sale. So in the search for objectivity, the accountants have settled for cost as the figure to record. It does mean that a balance sheet does not show the current worth or value of a business. That is not its intention. Nor does it mean that the 'cost' figure remains unchanged forever. For example, a motor car costing £6,000 may end up looking like this (Table 4.6) after two years:

Table 4.6 Example of the changing worth of an asset

Year 1		*Year 2*	
Fixed assets	£	Fixed assets	£
Motor car	6,000	Motor car	6,000
Less cumulative depreciation	1,500	*Less* cumulative depreciation	3,000
Net asset	4,500	Net asset	3,000

The depreciation is how we show the asset being 'consumed' over its working life. It is simply a bookkeeping record to allow us to allocate some of the cost of an asset to the appropriate time period. The time period will be determined by factors such as the working life of the asset. HMRC does not allow depreciation as a business expense – but it does allow tax relief on the capital expenditure. The proportion of capital purchase allowed by HMRC to be offset against tax is called the 'writing down' or 'capital allowance'. It is generally 25 per cent of the declining balance; in other words, in year one you can write down £250 on a capital purchase of £1,000, in year two £188 (25 per cent of £750) and so on. However, currently small and medium-sized firms are allowed to write down 40 per cent (but not on cars or assets for leasing). This measure was intended to stimulate capital expenditure.

Other assets, such as freehold land and buildings, will be revalued from time to time, and stock will be entered at cost, or market value, whichever is the lower, in line with the principle of conservatism (explained on page 46).

4. *Going concern.* Accounting reports always assume that a business will continue trading indefinitely into the future – unless there is good evidence to the contrary. This means that the assets of the business are looked at simply as profit generators and not as being available for sale.

   Look again at the motor car example above. In year 2, the net asset figures in the accounts, prepared on a 'going concern' basis, is £3,000. If we knew that the business was to close down in a few weeks, then we would be more interested in the car's resale value than its 'book' value: the car might fetch only £2,000, which is quite a different figure.

   Once a business stops trading, we cannot realistically look at the assets in the same way. They are no longer being used in the business to help generate sales and profits. The most objective figure is what they might realise in the marketplace. Anyone who has been to a sale of machinery will know the difference between book and market value!

5. *Dual aspect.* To keep a complete record of any business transaction we need to know both where money came from and what has been done with it. It is not enough simply to say, for example, that someone has put £1,000 into their business. We have to see how that money has been used.

   Take a look at the example in Table 4.7. Column 1 contains the figures we inherited before the owner put an extra £1,000 into the business. Column 2 shows what happened to the 'financed by' section of the balance sheet at the moment more money was put in. But as you can see, the balance sheet does not balance. It is also logically clear that we must have done something with that £1,000 the moment we received it. Column 3 shows exactly how we have used the money. It is tied up in cash. It could just as easily have been used to finance more customers (debtors) or to buy more stock, or even to pay off a bill, ie reduce creditors.

Table 4.7 An example of balance sheet changes

	1		2		3	
Net assets employed	£	£	£	£	£	£
Fixed assets		12,800		12,800		12,800
Current assets						
Stock	700		700		700	
Debtors	700		700		700	
Cash	400		400		1,400	
	1,800		1,800		2,800	
Less current liabilities						
Creditors	(900)		(900)		(900)	
Net current assets		900		900		1,900
		13,700		13,700		14,700
Financed by						
Owner's capital (less drawings)		7,000		8,000		8,000
10-year loan from bank		6,700		6,700		6,700
		13,700		14,700		14,700

However, the essential relationship of 'Assets = Capital + Liabilities' has to be maintained. That is the basis of double-entry bookkeeping. You can think of it as the accounting equivalent of Newton's third law: 'For every force there is an equal and opposite reaction'.

There are two other important accounting concepts, realisation and accrual, but they can be better dealt with when the next accounting report is looked at.

Accounting conventions

These concepts provide a useful set of ground rules, but they are open to a range of possible interpretations. Over time, a generally accepted approach to how the concepts are applied has been arrived at. This approach hinges on the use of three conventions: conservatism, materiality and consistency.

Conservatism

Accountants are often viewed as merchants of gloom, always prone to take a pessimistic point of view. The fact that a point of view has to be taken at all is the root of the problem. The convention of conservatism means that, given a choice, the accountant takes the figure that will result in a lower end profit. This might mean, for example, taking the higher of two possible expense figures. Few people are upset if the profit figure at the end of the day is higher than earlier estimates. The converse is never true.

Materiality

A strict interpretation of depreciation (see cost concept, item 3, on page 43) would lead to all sorts of trivial paperwork. For example, pencil sharpeners, staplers and paperclips, all theoretically items of fixed assets, should be depreciated over their working lives. This is obviously a useless exercise and in practice these items are written off when they are bought.

Clearly, the level of 'materiality' is not the same for all businesses. A multinational may not keep meticulous records of every item of machinery under £1,000. For a small business this may represent all the machinery it has.

Consistency

Even with the help of those concepts and conventions, there is a fair degree of latitude in how you can record and interpret financial information. You should choose the methods that give the fairest picture of how the firm is performing and stick with them. It is very difficult to keep track of events in a business that is always changing its accounting methods. This does not mean that you are stuck with one method for ever. Any change, however, is an important step.

The balance sheet shown earlier, though very simple, is complete enough to demonstrate the key principles involved. A much larger or more complex business may have more account categories, but the main sections of its balance sheet will be much the same, and you will now be able to recognize them.

Accounting for stock

Deciding on a figure to put into a balance sheet is a tricky calculation. Theoretically it is simple; after all, you know what you paid for it. The rule that stock should be entered in the balance sheet at cost or market price, whichever is the lower, is also not too difficult to follow. But in the real world a business keeps on buying in stock so it has product to sell and the cost can vary every time a purchase is made.

Take the example of a business selling a breakfast cereal. Four pallets of cereal are bought in from various suppliers at prices of £1,000, £1,020, £1,040 and £1,060 respectively, a total of £4,120. At the end of the period three pallets have been sold, so logically the cost of goods sold in the profit-and-loss account will show a figure of £3,060 (£1,000 + £1,020 + £1,040). The last pallet costing £1,060 will be the figure to put into the balance sheet, thus ensuring that all £4,120 of total costs are accounted for.

This method of dealing with stock is known as FIFO (first in first out), for obvious reason. There are two other popular costing methods that have their own merits. LIFO (last in first out) is based on the argument that if you are staying in business you will have to keep on replacing stock at the latest (higher) price, so you might just as well get used to that sooner by accounting for it in your profit and loss account. In this case the cost of goods sold would be £3,120 (£1,060 + £1,040 + £1,020), rather than the £3,060 that FIFO produces.

The third popular costing method is the average cost method, which does what it says on the box. In the above example this would produce a cost midway between that obtained by the other two methods, ie £3,090.

All these methods have their merits, but FIFO usually wins the argument as it accommodates the realities that prices rise steadily and goods move in and out of a business in the order in which they are bought. It would be a very badly run grocer's that sold its last delivery of cereal before clearing out the existing stocks.

Methods of depreciation

The depreciation is how we show the asset being 'consumed' over its working life. It is simply a bookkeeping record to allow us to allocate some of the cost of an asset to the appropriate time period. The time period will be determined by such factors as how long the working life of the asset is. The principal methods of depreciation used in business are:

- *The straight-line method.* This assumes that the asset will be 'consumed' evenly throughout its life. If, for example, an asset is being bought for £1,200 and sold at the end of five years for £200, the amount of cost we have to write off is £1,000. Using 20 per cent so that the whole 100 per cent of cost is allocated we can work out the 'book value' for each year.
- *The declining balance method.* This works in a similar way, but instead of an even depreciation each year we assume the drop will be less. Some assets, motor vehicles for example, will reduce sharply in their first year and less so later on. So while at the end of year one both these methods of depreciation will result in a £200 fall, in year two the picture starts to change. The straight-line method takes a further fall of £200, whilst the declining balance method reduces by 20 per cent (our agreed depreciation rate) of £800 (the balance of £1,000 minus the £200 depreciation so far), which is £160.
- *The sum-of-the-digits method.* This is more common in the United States than in the United Kingdom. While the declining balance method applies a constant percentage to a declining figure, this method applies a progressively smaller percentage to the initial cost. It involves adding up the individual numbers in the expected lifespan of the asset to arrive at the denominator of a fraction. The numerator is the year number concerned, but in reverse order. For example, if our computer asset bought for £1,200 had an expected useful life of five years (unlikely), then the denominator in our sum would be 1 + 2 + 3 + 4 + 5, which equals 15. In year one we would depreciate by $\frac{5}{15}$ of the initial purchase price of £1,200, which equals £400. In year two we would depreciate by $\frac{4}{15}$ths and so on.

These are just three of the most common of many ways of depreciating fixed assets. In choosing which method of depreciation to use, and in practice you may have to use different methods with different types of asset, it is useful to remember what you are trying to do. You are aiming to allocate the cost of buying the asset as it should apply to each year of its working life.

The capital register

One of the books you will keep will be a capital register, keeping track of the cost and depreciation of all fixed assets. Another accounting rule, that of 'materiality', comes into force here. Technically a pocket calculator costing

£5 is a fixed asset in that it has been bought to use rather than sell and it has a life of over one year. But it is treated as an expense, as the sum involved is too small to be material. There are no clear rules on the point at which a cost becomes material. For a big organization it may be for items costing a few thousands of pounds. For a small business £100 may be the appropriate level.

Preparing a package of accounts

The cash flow statement, the profit-and-loss account and the balance sheet between them constitute a set of accounts, but conventionally two balance sheets, the opening one and the closing one, are provided to make a 'package'. By including these balance sheets we can see the full picture of what has happened to the owner's investment in the business.

Table 4.8 shows a simplified package of accounts. We can see from these that over the year the business has made £600 of profit after tax, invested that in £200 of additional fixed assets and £400 of working capital such as stock and debtors, balancing that off with the £600 put into reserves from the year's profits.

Table 4.8 A package of accounts

Balance sheet at 31 Dec 07		P&L for year to 31 Dec 08		Balance sheet at 31 Dec 08	
	£		£		£
Fixed assets	1,000	Sales	10,000	Fixed assets	1,200
Working capital	1,000	Less cost of sales	6,000	Working capital	1,400
	2,000	Gross profit	4,000		2,600
		Less expenses	3,000		
Financed by		Profit before tax	1,000	Financed by	
Owner's equity	2,000	Tax	400	Owner's equity	2,000
		Profit after tax	600	Reserves	600
					2,600

Balance sheet and other online tools

SCORE (www.score.org > Business tools > Template gallery > Balance sheet (projected)) is an Excel-based spreadsheet you can use for constructing your own balance sheet. You can find guidance on depreciation and handling stock and on the layout of the balance sheet and profit-and-loss account as required by the Companies.Act from the Accounting Standards Board (www.frc.org.uk > ASB > Technical > FRSSE). Accounting Glossary (www.accountingglossary.net) and Accounting for Everyone (www.accountingforeveryone.com > Accounting glossary) have definitions of all the accounting terms you are ever likely to come across in the accounting world.

2

Understanding the figures

Cash is King in business – a debt management guide from Lloyds TSB Commercial

Debt management is absolutely essential to the smooth running of any firm's finances. It begins when you first consider selling products or services to a client and finishes when full payment has been received from that particular customer.

One of the golden rules of business is that a sale is not a sale until you have been paid. No matter how big or small your business is, it's your right to be paid on time. However, good credit control doesn't just happen – you need to work at it and get a good system in place.

The first stage of any debt management process, before you even take the first order, is to research formally or informally, the business background of any significant new client or customer you're dealing with. Always follow up references from your customer's existing suppliers and before offering a line of credit, have a look at their track record by performing a credit check. It is also important to set, and stick to, an appropriate limit. Don't be tempted to increase that limit until the customer has built up a good track record and you should also ask for a purchase order with each request as some businesses will refuse to pay your invoice without one.

Speeding up the payment process

In an ideal world, the best way to avoid payment problems is to ask for cash in advance or on delivery. This isn't always an option and not that many companies can achieve such payment terms. Alternatively, aim to receive all payments electronically – the money will get into your account more quickly and more securely. It is also sensible to get a feel for the standard payment time in your market – typical terms are 30, 60 or 90 days.

Make sure you also provide your customer with all the information they need to be able to pay you quickly and easily, such as your bank details for electronic payments. If you are supplying goods or services on a staged basis, ask your bank for a standing order form and consider offering these payment methods when doing business.

By ensuring all new customers clearly understand your payment terms, and with a clear agreement in place at the outset, you hold the cards when it comes to chasing payment. It is worth getting to know how the payment system works within your customers' businesses and exactly who is responsible for drawing cheques and making payments.

Another way of securing monies owed is to offer prompt payment discounts. Be careful how big you make the discount as being too generous will eat into profit margins.

When it comes to invoicing, Lloyds TSB Commercial recommends adopting these five simple, but, important habits:

1. invoice as soon as possible
2. include the customer's purchase order number
3. name the member of your staff who took the order as well as your contact details
4. delays cost you time and money, so, check each invoice for errors or omissions
5. follow up significant invoices by phone to check the customer is happy with them, you don't want to find out they are disputing something on the day the money is due for payment.

What to do if others fail to pay

When faced with a late payer, the key is to chase payments as soon as they become overdue and keep chasing and pressing for what you are owed. Start with phone calls and if this fails, put your claim in hand writing.

Make the first call and ask in a friendly, polite tone when you can expect to receive the overdue payment. Log every phone call and other contact you make chasing the payment, noting down who you spoke to, the time and date of the call, and details of the conversation. Confirm every phone call in writing.

Keep an up-to-date list of debtors at hand so you know when each debt becomes due. Then, if the customer calls to place another order, you can use this as leverage to ask for payment on the outstanding invoice. If you do run into problems be prepared to stop supplying further goods or services to the customer if they have not paid by the set time.

If phone calls get you nowhere, send a letter. In your first letter, state that you are disappointed not to have received the payment as promised in your telephone conversations. Draw attention to your terms and conditions regarding payment, which the customer agreed to.

Don't let emotions get in the way – maintain a businesslike tone in all letters. If a second letter is needed, make it firmer. Include the details you've recorded of each phone call made and the reminder letters that you've sent. Never make idle threats, if you say you will pass the matter onto your solicitor or a debt collection agency, make sure you do so promptly.

If all else fails, then you can resort to commencing legal action in the small claims court. This is where you can pursue small claims up to a value of £5,000. For larger claims, it may be necessary to retain lawyers and draw on their experience when it comes to deciding how to proceed. And if a legal battle is looming, make sure you've kept your end of the original bargain. You can't expect people to pay if your service has failed to match expectations or if goods have been delivered late or are of poor quality.

No matter how effective your system is, it will not be risk free. You should look to spread your cashflow risk and avoid large exposure to any one or few customers. It might be worth considering if credit insurance, factoring or invoice discounting are right for your business.

Credit Insurance

Taking out credit insurance is a means of protecting yourself against non-payment. In return for payment of a premium, usually negotiated annually, the credit insurer will insure against non-payment due to a variety of risks. The credit insurer will normally expect to insure most of your sales, both to good and bad payers, and will agree trading credit limits up to which you can sell to your customers and benefit from the cover. Credit insurers also have access to a range of historical information on the payment behaviour of customers.

Invoice discounting and factoring

These are two commonly used means of avoiding payment problems. An invoice discounting company will pay advances against invoices, up to around 90 per cent of the invoice value. The credit risk, however, remains with you, the supplier. If the customer doesn't pay up, you'll still have to repay the advance to the invoice discounter.

Factoring is an extension of a traditional invoice discounting service. Factoring companies may also offer credit checking or control services, cash collection or debt chasing. They can even offer to take over your entire sales ledger almost as if they were a department of your firm. This is best for businesses that do not want to devote large amounts of time and effort to payment control.

Above all, you must take charge of your business's cashflow. Many small businesses are so busy trying to land or fulfil orders that they take their eye off the ball and forget to set up a proper system for turning a sale into real money. An effective and organised system will help you control your cashflow and encourage customers to pay on time.

From help with your day-to-day cashflow, to growing your business, Lloyds TSB Commercial can help find the financial solution to match your needs. Visit **www.lloydstsb.com/business** to find out more.

This article is produced for information only and should not be relied on as offering advice for any specific set of circumstances.

Lloyds TSB Commercial is a trading name of Lloyds TSB Bank plc and Lloyds TSB Scotland plc and serves customers with an annual turnover of up to £15M.

Authorised and regulated by the Financial Services Authority and signatories to the Banking Codes.

5

Funding strategies, safety and performance

There are many sources of funds available to businesses. However, not all of them are equally appropriate to all businesses at all times. These different sources of finance carry very different obligations, responsibilities and opportunities for profitable business. Having some appreciation of these differences will enable you to make an informed choice.

Most businesses initially and often throughout their entire existence confine their financial strategy to bank loans, either long-term or short-term, viewing the other financing methods as either too complex or too risky. In many respects the reverse is true. Almost every finance source other than banks will to a greater or lesser extent share some of the risks of doing business with the recipient of the funds.

Debt vs equity

All businesses have access to two fundamentally different sorts of money. Equity, or owner's capital, including retained earnings, is money that is not a risk to the business. If no profits are made, then the owner and other shareholders simply do not get dividends. They may not be pleased, but they cannot usually sue.

Debt capital is money borrowed by the business from outside sources; it puts the business at financial risk and is also risky for the lenders. In return for taking that risk they expect an interest payment every year, irrespective of the performance of the business. High gearing is the name given when a business has a high proportion of outside money to inside money. High gearing has considerable attractions to a business that wants to make high returns on shareholders' capital.

How gearing works

Table 5.1 shows an example of a business that is assumed to need £60,000 capital to generate £10,000 operating profits. Four different capital structures are considered. They range from all share capital (no gearing) at one end to nearly all loan capital at the other. The loan capital has to be 'serviced', that is interest of 12 per cent has to be paid. The loan itself can be relatively indefinite, simply being replaced by another one at market interest rates when the first loan expires.

Table 5.1 The effect of gearing on ROSC

		No gearing	*Average gearing*	*High gearing*	*Very high gearing*
		–	1:1	2:1	3:1
Capital structure		£	£	£	£
Share capital		60,000	30,000	20,000	15,000
Loan capital (at 12%)		–	30,000	40,000	45,000
Total capital		60,000	60,000	60,000	60,000
Profits					
Operating profit		10,000	10,000	10,000	10,000
Less interest on loan		None	3,600	4,800	5,400
Net profit		10,000	6,400	5,200	4,600
Return on share capital	=	10,000 / 60,000	6,400 / 30,000	5,200 / 20,000	4,600 / 15,000
	=	16.6%	21.3%	26%	30.7%
Times interest earned	=	N/A	10,000 / 3,600	10,000 / 4,800	10,000 / 5,400
	=	N/A	2.8X*	2.1X	1.8X

*X is a convention for 'times'.

Following the table through you can see that return on the shareholders' money (arrived at by dividing the profit by the shareholders' investment and multiplying by 100 to get a percentage) grows from 16.6 to 30.7 per cent by virtue of the changed gearing. If the interest on the loan were lower, the ROSC, the term used to describe return on shareholders' capital, would be even more improved by high gearing, and the higher the interest the lower the relative improvement in ROSC. So in times of low interest, businesses tend to go for increased borrowings rather than raising more equity, that is money from shareholders.

At first sight this looks like a perpetual profit-growth machine. Naturally shareholders and those managing a business whose bonus depends on shareholders' returns would rather have someone else 'lend' them the money for the business than ask shareholders for more money, especially if by doing so they increase the return investment. The problem comes if the business does not produce £10,000 operating profits. Very often a drop in sales of 20 per cent means that profits are halved. If profits were halved in this example, the business could not meet the interest payments on its loan. That would make the business insolvent, and so not in a 'sound financial position': in other words, failing to meet one of the two primary business objectives.

Bankers tend to favour 1:1 gearing as the maximum for a business, although they have been known to go much higher. As well as looking at the gearing, lenders will study the business's capacity to pay interest. They do this by using another ratio called 'times interest earned'. This is calculated by dividing the operating profit by the loan interest. It shows how many times the loan interest is covered, and gives the lender some idea of the safety margin. The ratio for this example is given at the end of Table 5.1. Once again rules are hard to make, but much less than 3X interest earned is unlikely to give lenders confidence. (See Chapter 6 for a comprehensive explanation of the use of ratios.)

Using your own resources

If the business you are looking to finance is your own venture, then you should first look to your own resources. This is usually easier to arrange, cheaper, quicker and less time-consuming than any other source of money. There is of course another important advantage in that if you don't tap into bank borrowing and the like you may get a better reception later on, once your business is up and running.

Going for redundancy

Between 120,000 and 150,000 people are made redundant every month in the United Kingdom. High levels of redundancy are a continuing feature of the industrial landscape as the pace of change continues to accelerate. If you are in employment and could be eligible for redundancy, this could be a way of financing your business. In any event if your business takes off you are likely to have your hands full. These are the key factors to consider:

- Are you eligible for redundancy? This is a complex area but the Citizens Advice Bureau (www.adviceguide.org.uk/index/life/employment/redundancy.htm) has a summarized guide to the topic with useful links to other information.
- The first £30,000 of redundancy payment is normally tax-free, and any sum above that level is taxed at your highest tax rate. Redundancy Help (www.redundancyhelp.co.uk/MonTax.htm) provides a guide to the taxation of redundancy payments.
- Your pension entitlement may be adversely affected if you draw your pension earlier than your designated retirement age The Association of British Insurers and the Financial Services Authority have a pension calculator (www.pensioncalculator.org), which you can use to see what will happen to a pension by paying in for fewer years and retiring early.

Dipping into savings

If you have any savings put aside for a rainy day, then you could also consider dipping into them now. You will need to discuss this with your financial adviser, as there may be penalties associated with cashing in insurance policies early, for example. The Association of Investment and Financial Advisers (www.aifa.net) can help you to find an adviser in the United Kingdom or abroad.

Remortgaging

If you bought your present home five years or more ago the chances are that you are sitting on a large amount of equity – the difference between the current market value of your house and the amount you still owe the mortgagor. You can dip into this equity by remortgaging for a higher sum and taking out some cash. You should be able to take out between 80 and 90 per cent of the equity, though this may mean paying between 0.5 per cent and 1 per cent more for the whole mortgage, as well as an arrangement fee of anything from £200 to £700. If you need a relatively small amount of finance or only need the money for a short period to finance working capital this is probably not the best option.

You will find a guide to the whole subject at Mortgage Sorter (www.mortgagesorter.co.uk > Remortgages), where you will also find a remortgage quote service. The banks also offer advice on this subject (www.barclays.co.uk > Mortgages > Remortgaging).

Using credit cards

Why would anyone pay 18 per cent interest when they could get a bank overdraft at a third of that cost? The simple answer is that banks put their borrowers through a fairly stringent credit check (see below), while credit card providers have built a large volume of defaulting customers into their margins. In other words, you are paying over the odds to get fairly easy money.

Use a credit card by all means for travel and the like. Keep one to hand as part of your contingency planning to handle financial emergencies. But this type of money should not become part of the core funding of any business. Money Supermarket.com (www.moneysupermarket.com > Money > Credit cards) has a comparison tool that lets you compare over 300 cards, and About Your Money (www.aboutyourmoney.co.uk > Credit cards > Business cards) has an A–Z listing of business credit card providers and a comparison of the interest rates and other charges.

Earning sweat equity

Just because you are starting a business doesn't mean that every other money-making option is closed off. The attraction to earning money rather than borrowing it is that it is interest-free and never has to be paid back, as it would if it were borrowed from a bank. The harder you work, the more you can earn and put into the business: hence the name 'sweat equity'.

Using a local exchange trading scheme (LETS)

Local exchange trading allows anyone who joins a scheme to offer skills or services, such as plumbing, gardening or the use of a photocopier, to other members. A price is agreed in whatever notional currency has been adopted, but no money changes hands. The system is more ambitious than straight barter. The provider receives a credit on his or her account kept by a local organiser, and a debit is marked up against the user. The person in credit can then set this against other services.

The benefits of using LETS are that you can start trading and grow with virtually no start-up capital. All you need is time and saleable skills – once you have 'sold' your wares, payment is immediate by way of a LETS credit. Also, using LETS means that the wealth is kept in the local community, which means customers in your area may be able to spend more with you. One of the keys to success in using LETS is to have an enterprising organizer who can produce, maintain and circulate a wide-ranging directory of LETS services and outlets. Find out from Letslink UK (www.letslinkuk.net) more about the system and how to find your nearest organizer.

Borrowing money

At one end of the financing spectrum are the various organizations that lend money to businesses. They all try hard to take little or no risk, but expect some reward irrespective of performance. They want interest payments on money lent, usually from day one. While they too hope the management is competent, they are more interested in securing a charge against any assets the business or its managers may own. At the end of the day (and that day can be sooner than the borrower expects), they want all their money back – no more and certainly no less. It would be more prudent to think of these organizations as people who will help you turn a proportion of an illiquid asset, such as property, stock in trade or customers who have not yet paid up, into a more liquid asset such as cash, but of course at some discount.

Using a bank

Banks are the principal, and frequently the only, source of finance for 9 out of every 10 new and small businesses. Firms around the world rely on banks for their funding. In the United Kingdom, for example, firms have borrowed nearly £55 billion from the banks, a substantial rise over the past few years. When this figure is compared with the £48 billion that firms have on deposit at any one time, the net amount borrowed is around £7 billion.

Bankers, and indeed any other sources of debt capital, are looking for asset security to back their loan and provide a near-certainty of getting their money back. They will also charge an interest rate that reflects current market conditions and their view of the risk level of the proposal.

Bankers like to speak of the 'five Cs' of credit analysis, factors they look at when they evaluate a loan request. When applying to a bank for a loan, be prepared to address the following points:

- *Character.* Bankers lend money to borrowers who appear honest and who have a good credit history. Before you apply for a loan, it makes sense to obtain a copy of your credit report and clean up any problems.
- *Capacity.* This is a prediction of the borrower's ability to repay the loan. For a new business, bankers look at the business plan. For an existing business, bankers consider financial statements and industry trends.
- *Collateral.* Bankers generally want a borrower to pledge an asset that can be sold to pay off the loan if the borrower lacks funds.
- *Capital.* Bankers scrutinize a borrower's net worth, the amount by which assets exceed debts.
- *Conditions.* Whether bankers give a loan can be influenced by the current economic climate as well as by the amount.

Finding a business banker

Usage among firms of telephone and internet banking has significantly increased over the past few years. In 1998, 16 per cent of firms used telephone banking, rising to 38 per cent by 2007. For internet banking the proportion has risen from 14 per cent to 34 per cent. Branch location seems less likely to be a significant factor to bank customers in the future, so you no longer have to confine your search for a bank to those with a branch nearby. All the major clearing banks offer telephone banking and internet services to their small business customers, or are in the process of doing so.

You can see a listing of business bank accounts at Find.co.uk, the finance website (www.find.co.uk > Banking > Commercial > Business banking), where the top six or so are star-rated and reviewed, as well as an A–Z listing. Move Your Account (www.moveyouraccount.co.uk > Business banking) offer a free service claiming to find you the best current banking deal for a small business. You have to complete a dozen questions online and await their response. Startups (www.startups.co.uk > Finance management > Business bank accounts) offer a range of advice and tips on opening or changing a business bank account and what charges to look out for. The British Banking Association (www.bba.moneyfacts.co.uk) have a business bank account finder tool that also lets you compare your present bank against any others you may choose.

Giving bank guarantees

Where the assets of a business are small, anyone lending it money may seek the added protection of requiring the owner to guarantee the loan personally. In the case of limited companies, this is in effect stripping away some of the protection that companies are supposed to afford the risk-taking owner manager. You should resist giving guarantees if at all possible. If you have to, then try to secure the guarantee against the specific asset concerned only and set clear conditions for the guarantee to come to an end, for example when your overdraft or borrowings go down to a certain level.

Remember, everything in business finance is negotiable, and your relationship with a bank is no exception. Banks are in competition too, so if yours is being unreasonably hard it may be time to move on. Obviously, to be able to move on, you need to have some advance notice of when the additional funds are needed. Rushing into a bank asking for extra finance from next week is hardly likely to inspire much confidence in your abilities as a strategic thinker. That is where your business plan will come into its own.

Overdrafts

The principal form of short-term bank funding is an overdraft, secured by a charge over the assets of the business. A little over a quarter of all bank finance for small firms is in the form of an overdraft. If you are starting out in a contract cleaning business, say, with a major contract, you need sufficient funds initially to buy the mop and bucket. Three months into the contract they will have been paid for, and so there is no point in getting a five-year bank loan to cover this, as within a year you will have cash in the bank and a loan with an early redemption penalty!

However, if your bank account does not get out of the red at any stage during the year, you will need to re-examine your financing. All too often companies utilise an overdraft to acquire long-term assets, and that overdraft never seems to disappear, eventually constraining the business.

The attraction of overdrafts is that they are very easy to arrange and take little time to set up. That is also their inherent weakness. The key words in the arrangement document are 'repayable on demand', which leaves the bank free to make and change the rules as it sees fit. (This term is under constant review, and some banks may remove it from the arrangement.) With other forms of borrowing, as long as you stick to the terms and conditions, the loan is yours for the duration. It is not so with overdrafts.

Term loans

Term loans, as long-term bank borrowings are generally known, are funds provided by a bank for a number of years.

The interest can be either variable, changing with general interest rates, or fixed for a number of years ahead. The proportion of fixed-rate loans has increased from a third of all term loans to around one in two. In some cases it may be possible to move between having a fixed interest rate and a variable one at certain intervals. It may even be possible to have a moratorium on interest payments for a short period, to give the business some breathing space. Provided the conditions of the loan are met in such matters as repayment, interest and security cover, the money is available for the period of the loan. Term loans differ from overdrafts in that the bank cannot pull the rug from under you if circumstances (or the local manager) change.

Just over a third of all term loans are for periods of greater than 10 years, and a quarter are for three years or less.

Government small firm loan guarantee schemes

These are operated by banks at the instigation of governments in the United Kingdom, Australia, the United States and elsewhere. These schemes guarantee loans from banks and other financial institutions for small businesses with viable business proposals that have tried and failed to obtain a conventional loan because of a lack of security. Loans are available for periods of between two and 10 years on sums from £5,000 to £250,000.

The government guarantees 70–90 per cent of the loan. In return for the guarantee, the borrower pays a premium of 1–2 per cent per year on the outstanding amount of the loan. The commercial aspects of the loan are a matter between the borrower and the lender.

Securing a small firms loan

You can find out more about the Small Firms Loan Guarantee Scheme that operates in the United Kingdom on the Business Link website (www.businesslink.gov.uk > Finance and grants > Borrowing > Loans and overdrafts) and which banks operate the scheme on the Department for Business, Enterprise and Regulatory Reform website (www.berr.gov.uk > Better business framework > Small business > Information for small business owners and entrepreneurs > Access to finance > Small Firms Loan Guarantee).

Money through credit unions

If you don't like the terms on offer from the high street banks, as the major banks are often known, you could consider forming your own bank. This is not quite as crazy an idea as it sounds. Credit unions formed by groups of business-people, both in business and aspiring to start up, have been around for decades in the United States, the United Kingdom and elsewhere. They have been an attractive option for people on low incomes, providing a cheap and convenient alternative to banks. Some self-employed people such as taxi drivers have also formed credit unions. They can then apply for loans to meet unexpected capital expenditure for repairs, refurbishments or technical upgrading.

The popularity of credit unions varies from country to country. In the United Kingdom, for example, fewer than one in 300 people belong to one, compared with more than one in three in Canada, Ireland and Australia. Certainly, few could argue about the attractiveness of an annual interest rate 30 per cent below that of the high street lenders, which is what credit unions aim for. Members have to save regularly to qualify for a loan, although there is no minimum deposit, and after 10 weeks members with a good track record can borrow up to five times their savings, although they must continue to save while repaying the loan. There is no set interest rate, but dividends are distributed to members from any surplus, usually about 5 per cent a year. This too compares favourably with bank interest on deposit accounts.

Finding a credit union

You can find more about credit unions and details of those operating in your area from the Association of British Credit Unions Limited (www.abcul.org). For credit unions in the United States and in countries from Australia to the West Indies see Credit Unions Online (www.creditunionsonline.com).

Leasing and hiring equipment

Physical assets such as cars, vans, computers, office equipment and the like can usually be financed by leasing them, rather as a house or flat may be rented. Alternatively, they can be bought on hire purchase. This leaves other funds free to cover the less tangible elements in your cash flow.

Leasing is a way of getting the use of vehicles, plant and equipment without paying the full cost all at once. Operating leases are taken out where you will use the equipment (for example, a car, photocopier, vending machine or kitchen equipment) for less than its full economic life. The lessor takes the risk of the equipment becoming obsolete, and assumes responsibility for repairs, maintenance and insurance. As you, the lessee, are paying for this service, it is more expensive than a finance lease, where you lease the equipment for most of its economic life and maintain and insure it yourself. Leases can normally be extended, often for fairly nominal sums, in the latter years.

Hire purchase differs from leasing in that you have the option to eventually become the owner of the asset, after a series of payments.

Finding a leasing company

The Finance and Leasing Association (www.fla.org > For businesses > Business finance directory) gives details of all UK-based businesses offering this type of finance. The website also has general information on terms of trade and a code of conduct. Euromoney (www.euromoneybooks.com > Leasing & asset finance > Books) produce an annual *World Leasing Yearbook* with details on 4,250 leasing companies worldwide, price £170. You can, however, see a listing of most of the country leasing associations free in the 'Contributors' listing on this site.

Discounting and factoring

Customers often take time to pay up. In the meantime you have to pay those who work for you and your less patient suppliers. So, the more you grow, the more funds you need. It is often possible to 'factor' your creditworthy customers' bills to a financial institution, receiving some of the funds as your goods leave the door, hence speeding up cash flow.

Factoring is generally only available to a business that invoices other business customers, either in its home market or internationally, for its services. Factoring can be made available to new businesses, although its services are usually of most value during the early stages of growth. It is an arrangement that allows you to receive up to 80 per cent of the cash due from your customers more quickly than they would normally pay. The factoring company in effect buys your trade debts and can also provide a debtor accounting and administration service. You will, of course, have to pay for factoring services. Having the cash before your customers pay will cost you a little more than normal overdraft rates. The factoring service will cost between 0.5 and 3.5 per cent of the turnover, depending on volume of work, the number of debtors, the average invoice amount and other related factors. You can get up to 80 per cent of the value of your invoice in advance, with the remainder paid when your customer settles up, less the various charges just mentioned.

If you sell direct to the public, sell complex and expensive capital equipment, or expect progress payments on long-term projects, then factoring is not for you. If you are expanding more rapidly than other sources of finance will allow, this may be a useful service that is worth exploring.

Invoice discounting is a variation on the same theme, where you are responsible for collecting the money from debtors; this is not a service available to new or very small businesses.

Finding an invoice discounter or factor

The Asset Based Finance Association (www.thefda.org.uk/public/membersList.asp) is the association representing the United Kingdom's 41 factoring and invoice discounting businesses. This link is to their directory of members. InFactor (www.infactor.co.uk), launched in April 2006, is an online service for comparing factoring services, to select the best value for money for your need.

Supplier credit

Once you have established creditworthiness, it may be possible to take advantage of trade credit extended by suppliers. This usually takes the form of allowing you anything from seven days to three months from receiving the goods before you have to pay for them. Even if you are allowed time to pay for goods and services, you will have to weigh carefully the benefit of taking this credit against the cost of losing any cash discounts offered. For example, if you are offered a 2.5 per cent discount for cash settlement, then this is a saving of £25 for every £1,000 of purchases. If the alternative is to take six weeks' credit, the saving is the cost of borrowing that sum from, say, your bank on overdraft. So, if your bank interest rate is 8 per cent per annum, that is equivalent to 0.15 per cent per week. Six weeks would save you 0.92 per cent. On £1,000 of purchases you would save only £9.20 of bank interest. This means that the cash discount is more attractive.

Checking your creditworthiness

However, your suppliers will probably run a credit check on you before extending payment terms. You should run a credit check on your own business from time to time, just to see how others see you. You can check out your own credit rating before trying to get credit from a supplier by using a credit reference agency such as Snoop4 Companies (www.snoop4companies.co.uk) for businesses or Experian (www.experian.co.uk) for sole traders. Basic credit reports cost between £3 and £25 and may save you time and money if you have any reservations about a potential customer's ability to pay.

Family and friends

Those close to you might be willing to lend you money or invest in your business. This helps you avoid the problem of pleading your case to outsiders and enduring extra paperwork and bureaucratic delays. Help from friends, relatives and business associates can be especially valuable if you have been through bankruptcy or had other credit problems that would make borrowing from a commercial lender difficult or impossible.

Their involvement brings a range of extra potential benefits, costs and risks that are not a feature of most other types of finance. You need to decide which of these are acceptable.

Some advantages of borrowing money from people you know well are that you may be charged a lower interest rate, may be able to delay paying back money until you are more established, and may be given more flexibility if you get into a jam. But once the loan terms are agreed to, you have the same legal obligations as you would with a bank or any other source of finance.

In addition, borrowing money from relatives and friends can have a major disadvantage. If your business does poorly and those close to you end up losing money, you may well damage a good personal relationship. So, in dealing with friends, relatives and business associates, be extra careful not only to establish clearly the terms of the deal and put them in writing but also to make an extra effort to explain the risks. In short, it is your job to make sure your helpful friend or relative will not suffer true hardship if you are unable to meet your financial commitments.

Getting an investor

If you are operating as a limited company or limited partnership you will have a potentially valuable opportunity to raise relatively risk-free money. It is risk-free to you, the business founder, that is, but risky, sometimes extremely so, to anyone advancing you money. Businesses such as these have shares that can be traded for money, so selling a share of your business is one way to raise capital to start up or grow your business. Shares also have the great additional attraction of having cost you nothing – nothing, that is, except blood, sweat, tears and inspiration.

Individual business angels, or corporates such as venture capital providers share all the risks and vagaries of the business alongside you, the founder, and expect a proportionate share in the rewards if things go well. They are not especially concerned with a stream of dividends, which is just as well, as few small businesses ever pay them. Nor do they look for the security of buildings or other assets to underpin their investment. Instead they hope for a radical increase in the value of their investment. They expect to realize this value from other investors who want to take their place for the next stage in the firm's growth cycle rather than from any repayment by the founder.

Business angels

One likely first source of equity or risk capital will be a private individual with his or her own funds and perhaps some knowledge of your type of business. In return for a share in the business, such investors will put in money at their own risk. They have been christened 'business angels', a term first coined to describe private wealthy individuals who back a play on Broadway or in London's West End.

Most angels are determined upon some involvement beyond merely signing a cheque and may hope to play a part in your business in some way. They are hoping for big rewards – one angel who backed Sage with £10,000 in its first round of £250,000 financing saw his stake rise to £40 million.

These angels frequently operate through managed networks, usually on the internet. In the United Kingdom and the United States there are hundreds of networks, with tens of thousands of business angels prepared to put up several billion pounds each year to new or small businesses.

Finding a business angel

The British Business Angels Association (www.bbaa.org.uk) has an online directory of UK business angels. The European Business Angels Network (EBAN) has directories of national business angel associations both inside and outside of Europe (www.eban.org > Members) from which you can find individual business angels.

Venture capital or private equity

Venture capital (VC) providers are investing other people's money, often from pension funds. They have a different agenda from that of business angels and are more likely to be interested in investing more money for a larger stake.

VCs go through a process known as 'due diligence' before investing. This process involves a thorough examination of both the business and its owners. Past financial performance, the directors' track record and the business plan are all subjected to detailed scrutiny, usually by accountants and lawyers. Directors are then required to 'warrant' that they have provided all relevant information, under pain of financial penalties. The cost of this process will have to be borne by the firm raising the money, but it will be paid out of the money raised, if that is any consolation.

In general, VCs expect their investment to have paid off within seven years, but they are hardened realists. Two in every 10 investments they make are total write-offs, and six perform averagely well at best. So, the one star in every 10 investments they make has to cover a lot of duds. VCs have a target rate of return of 30 per cent plus, to cover this poor hit rate.

Raising venture capital is not a cheap option, and deals are not quick to arrange either. Six months is not unusual, and over a year has been known. Every VC has a deal done in six weeks in its portfolio, but that truly is the exception.

Finding venture capital

The British Venture Capital Association (www.bvca.co.uk) and the European Venture Capital Association (www.evca.com) both have online directories giving details of hundreds of venture capital providers. The Australian government has a global venture capital directory on this website (www.austradeict.gov.au/Global-VC-directory/default.aspx), and the National Venture Capital Association in the United States has directories of international venture capital associations both inside and outside the United States (www.nvca.org > Resources).

You can see how those negotiating with or receiving venture capital rate the firm in question at The Funded website (www.thefunded.com) in terms of the deal offered, the firm's apparent competence and how good it is at managing the relationship. There is also a link to the VC's website. The Funded has 2,500 members.

Corporate venturing

Venture capital firms often get their hands dirty taking a hand in the management of the businesses they invest in. Another type of business is also in the risk capital business, without it necessarily being its main line of business. These firms, known as corporate venturers, usually want an inside track to new developments in and around the edges of their own fields of interest. For example, Microsoft, Cisco and Apple have billions of dollars invested in hundreds of small entrepreneurial firms, taking stakes from a few hundred thousand dollars up to hundreds of millions.

And it's not just high-tech businesses that take this approach. McDonald's held a 35 per cent stake in Pret A Manger whilst they worked out where to take their business after saturating the burger market. HM Revenue & Customs (www.hmrc.gov.uk/guidance/cvs.htm) has a useful guide entitled 'The Corporate Venturing Scheme', explaining the scheme and the tax implications and giving sources of further information.

Going public

Stock markets are the place where serious businesses raise serious money. It's possible to raise anything from a few million to tens of billions; expect the costs and efforts in getting listed to match those stellar figures. The basic idea is that owners sell shares in their businesses, which in effect brings in a whole raft of new 'owners', who in turn have a stake in the businesses' future profits. When they want out they sell their shares on to other investors. The share price moves up and down to ensure that there are as many buyers as sellers at any one time.

Going public also puts a stamp of respectability on you and your company. It will enhance the status and credibility of your business, and it will enable you to borrow more against the 'security' provided by your new shareholders, should you so wish. Your shares will also provide an attractive way to retain and motivate key staff. If they are given, or rather are allowed to earn, share options at discounted prices, they too can participate in the capital gains you are making. With a public share listing you can now join in the takeover and asset-stripping game. When your share price is high and things are going well you can look out for weaker firms to gobble up – and all you have to do is to offer them more of your shares in return for theirs. You do not even have to find real money. But of course this is a two-sided game, and you also may now become the target of a hostile bid.

You may find that being in the public eye not only cramps your style but fills up your engagement diary too. Most CEOs of public companies find that they have to spend up to a quarter of their time 'in the City', explaining their strategies, in the months preceding and the first years following their going public.

It is not unusual for so much management time to have been devoted to answering accountants' and stockbrokers' questions that there is not enough time to run the day-to-day business, and profits drop as a direct consequence.

The City also creates its own 'pressure' both to seduce companies on to the market and then by expecting them to perform beyond any reasonable expectation.

Criteria for getting a listing

The rules vary from market to market, but there are certain conditions that are likely to apply to get a company listed on an exchange.

Getting listed on a major stock exchange calls for a track record of making substantial profits with decent seven-figure sums being made in the year you plan to float, as this process is known. A listing also calls for a large proportion, usually at least 25 per cent, of the company's shares being put up for sale at the outset. In addition, you would be expected to have 100 shareholders now and be able to demonstrate that 100 more will come on board as a result of the listing.

As you draw up your flotation plan and timetable you should have the following matters in mind:

- *Advisers.* You will need to be supported by a team that will include a sponsor, stockbroker, reporting accountant and solicitor. These should be respected firms, active in flotation work and familiar with the company's type of business. You and your company may be judged by the company you keep, so choose advisers of good repute and make sure that the personalities work effectively together. It is very unlikely that a small local firm of accountants, however satisfactory, will be up to this task.
- *Sponsor.* You will need to appoint a financial institution, usually a merchant banker, to fill this important role. If you do not already have a merchant bank in mind, your accountant will offer guidance. The job of the sponsor is to coordinate and drive the project forward.
- *Timetable.* It is essential to have a timetable for the final months during the run-up to a float – and to adhere to it. The company's directors and senior staff will be fully occupied in providing information and attending meetings. They will have to delegate, and there must be sufficient back-up support to ensure that the business does not suffer.
- *Management team.* A potential investor will want to be satisfied that your company is well managed, at board level and below. It is important to ensure succession, perhaps by offering key directors and managers

service agreements and share options. It is wise to draw on the experience of well-qualified non-executive directors.

- Accounts. The objective is to have a profit record that is rising, but in achieving this you will need to take into account directors' remuneration, pension contributions and the elimination of any expenditure that might be acceptable in a privately owned company but would not be acceptable in a public company, namely excessive perks such as yachts, luxury cars, lavish expense accounts and holiday homes. Accounts must be consolidated and audited to appropriate accounting standards, and the audit reports must not contain any major qualifications. The auditors will need to be satisfied that there are proper stock records and a consistent basis of valuing stock during the years prior to flotation. Accounts for the past three years will need to be disclosed, and the date of the last accounts must be within six months of the issue.

Using AIM

London's Alternative Investment Market (AIM) was formed in the mid-1990s specifically to provide risk capital for new rather than established ventures. AIM raised £15.7 billion in 2007 – a 76 per cent leap from the previous year – and a record number of companies floated on the exchange, bringing the total to 1,634.

AIM is particularly attractive to any dynamic company of any size, age or business sector that has rapid growth in mind. The smallest firm on AIM entered at under £1 million capitalization and the largest at over £500 million. The formalities are minimal, but the costs of entry are high and you must have a nominated adviser, such as a major accountancy firm, stockbroker or banker. The survey showed that costs of floating on the junior market are around 6.5 per cent of all funds raised, and companies valued at less than £2 million can expect to shell out a quarter of funds raised in costs alone. The market is regulated by the London Stock Exchange (www.londonstockexchange.com > AIM).

You can check out all the world stock markets from Australia to Zagreb at Stock Exchanges World Wide Links (www.tdd.lt/slnews/Stock_Exchanges/Stock.Exchanges.htm) maintained by Aldas Kirvaitis of Lithuania and at WorldWide-Tax.com (www.worldwide-tax.com > World stock exchanges). Once in the stock exchange website, almost all of which have pages in English, look out for a term such as 'Listing center', 'Listing' or 'Rules'. There you will find the latest criteria for floating a company on that particular exchange.

Free money

Strangely enough there is such a thing as a free lunch in the money world. It can come in the form of a benevolent government whose agenda is either to get businesses to locate in an area more full of sheep than customers or to pioneer new technologies. In addition businesses, newspapers and magazines run competitions galore and offer prizes to the best-run, fastest-growing or biggest-exporting business and so forth. For the sponsor the reward is publicity and good stories, and for the business founders there is money.

Gaining grants

Grants are constantly being introduced (and withdrawn), but there is no system that lets you know automatically. You have to keep yourself informed.

Business Link (www.businesslink.gov.uk > Finance and grants > Grants and government support) has advice on how to apply for a grant, as well as a directory of grants on offer. Microsoft Small Business Centre (www.microsoft.com/uk/businesscentral/euga/home.aspx) has a European Union Grant Advisor with a search facility to help you find which of the 6,000 grants on offer might suit your business needs. Grants.gov (www.grants.gov) is a guide to how to apply for over 1,000 federal government grants in the United States.

Winning competitions

There are thousands of annual awards around the world aimed at new or small businesses. Most are based around a business plan or other presentation of your business ideas. For the most part, these are sponsored by banks, the major accountancy bodies, chambers of commerce, local or national newspapers, business magazines, and the trade press. Government departments may also have their own competitions as a means of promoting their initiatives for exporting, innovation, job creation and so forth. There is a Business Plan Competition Directory on the Small Business Notes website, run by Judith Kautz (www.smallbusinessnotes.com/planning/competitions.html).

6

Using ratios

Just having the accounts of a business is not of much use in itself if you can't analyse and interpret them. The tools for measuring the relationship between various elements of performance to see whether we are getting better or worse are known as ratios; simply put, these involve expressing one thing as a proportion of another with a view to gaining an appreciation of what has happened. For example, miles per gallon is a measure of the efficiency of a motor vehicle. If that 'ratio' is 40 miles per gallon in one period and 30 miles per gallon in another it would be a cause for concern and investigation as to what had caused the drop in performance.

Ratios are used to compare performance in one period, say last month or year, with another – this month or year; they can also be used to see how well your business is performing compared with another, say a competitor's. You can also use ratios to compare how well you have done against your target or budget. In the financial field the opportunity for calculating ratios is great, for computing useful ratios not quite so great. These are the key ratios every business needs to keep track of.

Levels of profit

Look back to Table 3.2, where you can see High Note's profit performance in some detail. Using those figures, the following ratios are calculated below.

Gross profit

This is calculated by dividing the gross profit by sales and multiplying by 100. In this example, the sum is 30,000/60,000 × 100 = 50 per cent. This is a measure of the value we are adding to the bought-in materials and services we need to 'make' our product or service; the higher the figure the better.

Operating profit

This is calculated by dividing the operating profit by sales and multiplying by 100. In this example, the sum is 8,700/60,000 × 100 = 14.5 per cent. This is a measure of how efficiently we are running the business, before taking account of financing costs and tax. These are excluded, as interest and tax rates change periodically and are outside our direct control. Excluding them makes it easier to compare one period with another or with another business. Once again the rule here is the higher the figure the better.

Net profit before and after tax

This is calculated by dividing the net profit before and after tax by the sales and multiplying by 100. In this example, the sums are 8,100/60,000 × 100 = 13.5 per cent and 6,723/60,000 × 100 = 11.21 per cent. This is a measure of how efficiently we are running the business, after taking account of financing costs and tax. The last figure shows how successful we are at creating additional money either to invest back in the business or to distribute to the owner(s) as either drawings or dividends. Once again the rule here is the higher the figure the better.

Working capital relationships

The money tied up in day-to-day activities is known as working capital, the sum of which is arrived at by subtracting the current liabilities from the current assets. In the case of High Note (Table 4.5) we have £21,108 in current assets and £4,908 in current liabilities, so the working capital is £16,200.

Current ratio

As a figure the working capital doesn't tell us much. It is rather as if you knew your car had used 20 gallons of petrol but had no idea how far you had travelled. It would be more helpful to know how much larger the current assets are than the current liabilities. That would give us some idea if the funds would be available to pay bills for stock, the tax liability and any other short-term liabilities that may arise. The current ratio, which is arrived at by dividing the current assets by the current liabilities, is the measure used. For High Note this is 21,108/4,908 = 4.30. The convention is to express this as 4.30:1 and the aim here is to have a ratio of between 1.5:1 and 2:1. Any lower and bills can't be met easily and much higher and money is being tied up unnecessarily.

Average collection period

We can see that High Note's current ratio is high, which is an indication that some elements of working capital are being used inefficiently. The business has £12,000 owed by customers on sales of £60,000 over a six-month period. The average period it takes High Note to collect money owed is calculated by dividing the sales made on credit by the money owed and multiplying it by the time period in days; in this case the sum is as follows: 12,000/60,000 × 182.5 = 36.5 days.

If the credit terms are cash with order or seven days, then something is going seriously wrong. If it is net 30 days then it is probably about right. In this example it has been assumed that all the sales were made on credit.

Days' stock held

High Note is carrying £9,108 stock of sheet music, CDs, etc, and over the period it sold £30,000 of stock at cost. (The cost of sales is £30,000 to support £60,000 of invoiced sales, as the mark-up in this case is 100 per cent.) Using a similar sum as with average collection period we can calculate that the stock being held is sufficient to support 55.41 days' sales (9,108/30,000 × 182.5). If High Note's suppliers can make weekly deliveries then this is almost certainly too high a stock figure to hold. Cutting stock back from nearly eight weeks (55.41 days) to one week (7 days) would trim 48.41 days or £7,957.38 worth of stock out of working capital. This in turn would bring the current ratio down to 2.68:1.

Return on investment (ROI)

The fundamental financial purpose in business is to make a satisfactory return on the funds invested. Return on investment is calculated as a percentage in the same way as the interest you would get on any money on deposit in a bank would be. In High Note £28,700 has been put into the business from various sources including the bank, to generate an operating profit of £8,700, that is profit before we pay the bank interest on money owed or tax. The return is calculated as 8,700/28,700 × 100 = 30.31 per cent.

Appreciating gearing

The return on investment ratio is arrived at taking into account all the sources of money used. However, High Note's owner has only £10,000 of his or her own money invested, and the profit made after paying bank interest of £600 is £8,100. So the return on the owner's investment is 8,100/10,000 × 100 = 81 per cent, which by any standards is acceptable.

If the owner had been able to get an overdraft of £15,000 rather than the £10,000 secured and so put in only £5,000 of his or her own cash the return on the investment would have been better still. Interest cost would increase to £900, so profit after interest would drop to £7,800, but the owner's investment being just £5,000 means that the return on the investment would rise to 156 per cent (7,800/5,000 × 100).

There is a limit to the amount of money a bank will put up compared to the amount an owner puts in. Typically banks will look to no more than match pound for pound the owner's funding, and in any event they will want to secure their loan against some tangible asset such as a property.

Market tests

This is the name given to stock market measures of performance for companies listed on stock markets. Four key ratios here are earnings per share (EPS), price earnings ratio (P/E), yield and dividend cover:

1. Earnings per share = Net profit : Shares outstanding.
   This is the after-tax profit made by a company divided by the number of ordinary shares it has issued.
2. Price earnings ratio = Market price per share : Earnings per share.
   Here the market price of an ordinary share is divided by the earnings per share. The PE ratio expresses the market value placed on the expectation of future earnings, ie the number of years required to earn the price paid for the shares out of profits at the current rate.

3. Yield = Dividends per share : Price per share.
   This is the percentage return a shareholder gets on the 'opportunity' value of the investment, ie what the shareholder could get by selling the shares now.
4. Dividend cover = Net income : Dividend.
   This is the number of times the profit exceeds the dividend; the higher the ratio, the more retained profit to finance future growth.

Combined ratios

No one would use a single ratio to decide whether one vehicle was a better or worse buy than another. MPG, MPH, annual depreciation percentage and residual value proportion are just a handful of the ratios that would need to be reviewed. So it is with a business. These combinations of ratios can be used to form an opinion on the financial state of affairs at any one time.

The best known of these combination ratios is the Altman Z-Score (www.creditguru.com/CalcAltZ.shtml), which uses a combined set of five financial ratios derived from eight variables from a company's financial statements linked to some statistical techniques to predict a company's probability of failure. Entering the figures into the on-screen template at this website produces a score and an explanatory narrative giving a view on the business's financial strengths and weaknesses.

Getting company accounts

It will be very useful to look at other comparable businesses to see their ratios as a yardstick against which to compare your own business's performance. For publicly quoted and larger businesses whose accounts are audited this should not be too difficult. However, for smaller private companies the position is not quite so simple. In the first place small companies, that is those with an annual turnover below £5.6 million, a balance sheet total below £2.8 million and employing fewer than 50 staff, need only file an abbreviated balance sheet. Even medium-sized businesses with turnover up to £22.8 million can omit turnover from the information filed on their financial performance. Only public companies listed on a stock market and larger companies have to provide full financial statements.

Despite the limitation it is still possible to glean some valuable information on financial performance using these sources:

- Companies House (www.companieshouse.gov.uk) is the official repository of all company information in the United Kingdom. Their WebCHeck service offers a free-of-charge searchable company names and addresses index, which covers 2 million companies by either name or unique company registration number. You can use WebCHeck to purchase a company's latest accounts, giving details of sales, profits, margins, directors, shareholders and bank borrowings, at a cost of £1 per company.
- Credit reports such as those provided by www.ukdata.com, www.checksure.biz, www.business-inc.co.uk cost around £8, are available online and provide basic business performance ratios.
- FAME (Financial Analysis Made Easy) is a powerful database that contains information on 3.4 million companies in the United Kingdom and Ireland. Typically the following information is included: contact information including phone, e-mail and web addresses plus main and other trading addresses, activity details, 29 profit-and-loss account and 63 balance sheet items, cash flow and ratios, credit score and rating, security and price information (listed companies only), names of bankers, auditors, previous auditors and advisers, details of holdings and subsidiaries (including foreign holdings and subsidiaries), names of current and previous directors with home addresses and shareholder indicator, heads of department, and shareholders. You can compare each company with detailed financials with its peer group based on its activity codes, and the software lets you search for companies that comply with your own criteria, combining as many conditions as you like. FAME is available in business libraries and on CD from the publishers, who also offer free trial (www.bvdep.com/en/companyInformationHome.html > Company data – national > FAME).
- Keynote (www.keynote.co.uk) operates in 18 countries, providing business ratios and trends for 140 industry sectors to assess accurately the financial health of each industry sector. Using this service you can find out how profitable a business sector is and how the successful the main companies operating in each sector are. Executive summaries are free, but expect to pay between £250 and £500 for most reports.
- London Stock Exchange's website (www.londonstockexchange.com).
- Proshare (www.proshareclubs.co.uk > Research centre >Performance tables) is an investment club website. Once you have registered, which you can do free, it has a number of tools that crunch public company ratios for you. Select the companies you want to look at and then the ratios you are most interested in: EPS, P/E, ROI, dividend yield and so

forth. Press the button and in a couple of seconds all is revealed. You can then rank the companies by performance in more or less any way you want.

- Yahoo (http://uk.finance.yahoo.com > Free annual reports) has direct links to several thousand public companies' reports and accounts online, so you can save yourself the time and trouble of hunting down company websites.

Ratio analysis spreadsheets

Bookkeeping and accounting software often has 'report generator' programs that crunch out ratios for you, sometimes with helpful suggestions on areas to be probed further. Biz/ed (www.bized.co.uk > Company information > Financial ratio analysis) and the Harvard Business School (http://harvardbusinessonline.hbsp.harvard.edu/b02/en/academic/edu_tk_acct_fin_ratio.jhtml) have free tools that calculate financial ratios from your financial data. They also provide useful introductions to ratio analysis as well as defining each ratio and the formula used to calculate it. You need to register on the Harvard website to be able to download their spreadsheet.

7

Costs, volume, pricing and profit decisions

In the preceding chapters we have seen how business controls can be developed. These can be used to monitor performance against the fundamental objectives of profitability, and the business's capacity to survive. So far we have taken certain decisions for granted and ignored how to cost the product or service we are marketing, and, indeed, how to set the selling price. These decisions are clearly very important if you want to be sure of making a profit.

Adding up the costs

At first glance the problem is simple. You just add up all the costs and charge a bit more. The more you charge above your costs, provided the customers will keep on buying, the more profit you make.

Unfortunately as soon as you start to do the sums the problem gets a little more complex. For a start, not all costs have the same characteristics. Some costs, for example, do not change however much you sell. If you are running a shop, the rent and rates are relatively constant figures, completely independent of the volume of your sales. On the other hand, the cost of the products sold from the shop is completely dependent on volume. The more you sell, the more it costs you to buy in stock.

	£
Rent and rates for shop	2,500
Cost of 1,000 units of volume of product	1,000
Total costs	3,500

You can't really add up those two types of costs until you have made an assumption about volume – how much you plan to sell.

Look at the simple example above. Until we decide to buy, and we hope sell, 1,000 units of our product, we cannot total the costs.

With the volume hypothesised we can arrive at a cost per unit of product of:

Total costs	÷ Number of units	
= £3,500	÷ 1,000	= £3.50

Now, provided we sell out all the above at £3.70, we shall always be profitable. But will we? Suppose we do not sell all the 1,000 units, what then? With a selling price of £4.50 we could, in theory, make a profit of £1,000 if we sell all 1,000 units. That is a total sales revenue of £4,500, minus total costs of £3,500. But if we only sell 500 units, our total revenue drops to £2,250 and we actually lose £1,250* (total revenue £2,250 – total costs £3,500). So at one level of sales a selling price of £4.50 is satisfactory, and at another it is a disaster.

This very simple example shows that all those decisions are intertwined. Costs, sales volume, selling prices and profits are all linked together. A decision taken in any one of these areas has an impact on the other areas.

To understand the relationship between these factors, we need a picture or model of how they link up. Before we can build up this model, we need some more information on each of the component parts of cost.

The components of cost

Understanding the behaviour of costs as the trading patterns in a business change is an area of vital importance to decision makers. It is this 'dynamic' nature in every business that makes good costing decisions the key to survival. The last example showed that if the situation was static and predictable, a profit was certain, but that if any one component in the equation was not a certainty (in that example it was volume), then the situation was quite different.

To see how costs behave under changing conditions we first have to identify the different types of cost.

* The loss may not be as dramatic as that because we may still have the product available to sell later, but if it is fresh vegetables, for example, we will not. In any event, stored products attract new costs, such as warehousing and finance charges.

Fixed costs

Fixed costs are costs that happen, by and large, whatever the level of activity. For example, the cost of buying a car is the same whether it is driven 100 miles a year or 20,000 miles. The same is also true of the road tax, the insurance and any extras, such as a radio.

In a business, as well as the cost of buying cars, there are other fixed costs such as plant, equipment, computers, desks, and telephones. But certain less tangible items can also be fixed costs, for example, rent, rates, insurance, etc, which are usually set quite independent of how successful or otherwise a business is.

Costs such as most of those mentioned above are fixed irrespective of the timescale under consideration. Other costs, such as those of employing people, while theoretically variable in the short term, in practice are fixed. In other words, if sales demand goes down and a business needs fewer people, the costs cannot be shed for several weeks (notice, holiday pay, redundancy, etc). Also, if the people involved are highly skilled or expensive to recruit and train (or in some other way particularly valuable) and the downturn looks a short one, it may not be cost-effective to reduce those short-run costs in line with falling demand. So viewed over a period of weeks and months, labour is a fixed cost. Over a longer period it may not be fixed.

We could draw a simple chart showing how fixed costs behave as the 'dynamic' volume changes. The first phase of our cost model is shown overleaf (Figure 7.1).

This shows a static level of fixed costs over a particular range of output. To return to a previous example, this could show the fixed cost, rent and rates for a shop to be constant over a wide range of sales levels.

Once the shop owner has reached a satisfactory sales and profit level in one shop, he or she may decide to rent another one, in which case the fixed costs will 'step' up. This can be shown in the variation on the fixed cost model in Figure 7.2.

Variable costs

These are costs that change in line with output. Raw materials for production, packaging materials, bonuses, piece rates, sales commission and postage are some examples. The important characteristic of a variable cost is that it rises or falls in direct proportion to any growth or decline in output volumes.

We can now draw a chart showing how variable costs behave as volume changes. The second phase of our cost model will look like Figure 7.3.

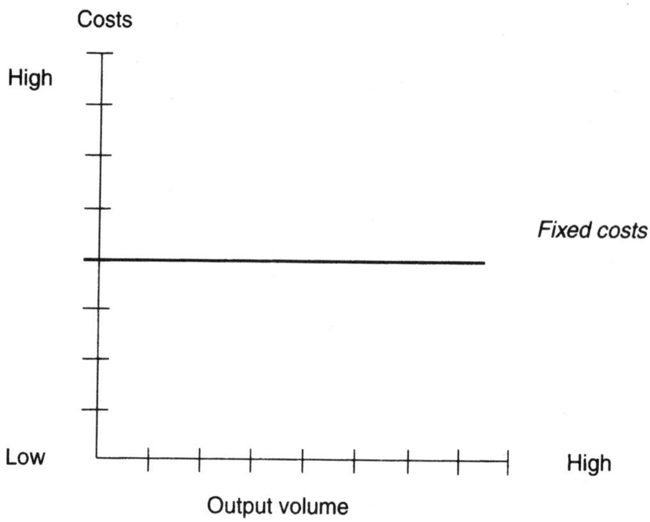

Figure 7.1 Cost model 1: showing fixed costs

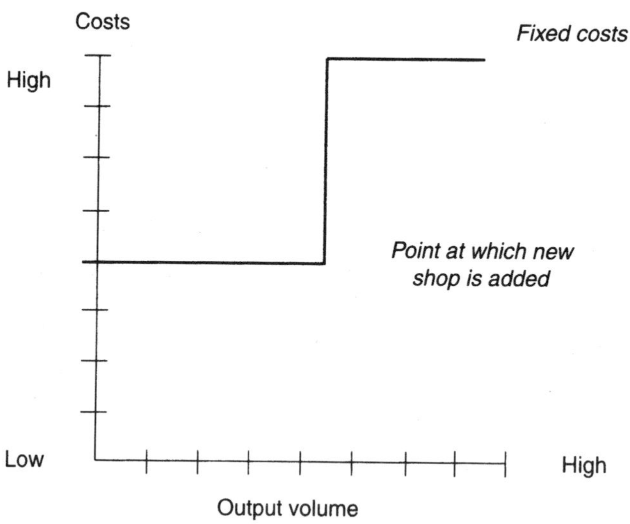

Figure 7.2 Variation on cost model 1: showing a 'step up' in fixed costs

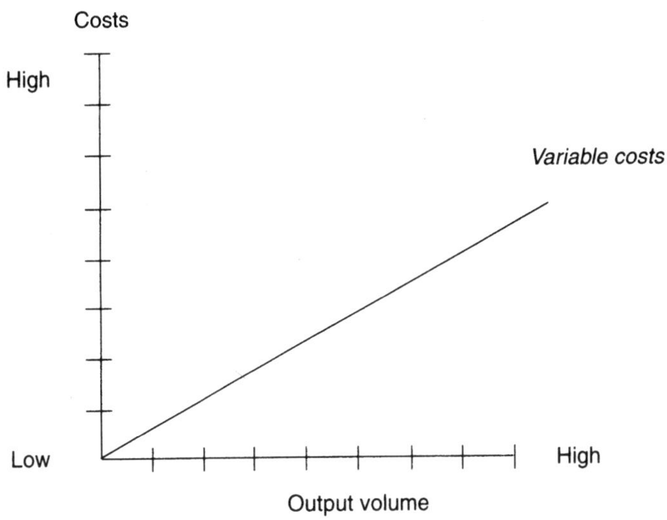

Figure 7.3 Cost model 2: showing behaviour of variable costs as volume changes

There is a popular misconception that defines fixed costs as those costs that are predictable, and variable costs as those that are subject to change at any moment. The definitions already given are the only valid ones for costing purposes.

Semi-variable costs

Unfortunately not all costs fit easily into either the fixed or variable category.

Some costs have both a fixed and a variable element. For example, a telephone has a quarterly rental cost which is fixed, and a cost per unit consumed which is variable. In this particular example low consumers can be seriously penalised. If only a few calls are made each month, their total cost per call (fixed rental + cost per unit ÷ number of calls) can be several pounds.

Other examples of this dual-component cost are photocopier rentals, electricity and gas.

These semi-variable costs must be split into their fixed and variable elements. For most small businesses this will be a fairly simple process; nevertheless it is essential to do it accurately or else much of the purpose and benefits of this method of cost analysis will be wasted.

Break-even point

Now we can bring both these phases of the costing model together to show the total costs, and how they behave (Figure 7.4).

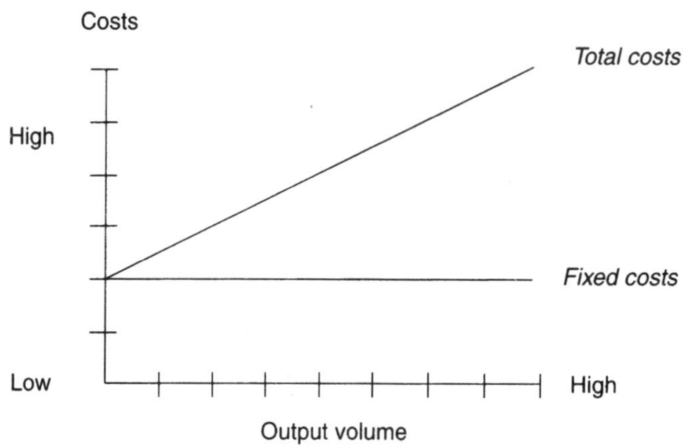

Figure 7.4 Cost model showing total costs and fixed costs

By starting the variable costs from the plateau of the fixed costs, we can produce a line showing the total costs. Taking vertical and horizontal lines from any point in the total cost line will give the total costs for any chosen output volume. This is an essential feature of the costing model that lets us see how costs change with different output volumes: in other words, accommodating the dynamic nature of a business.

It is to be hoped that we are not simply producing things and creating costs. We are also selling things and creating income. So a further line can be added to the model to show sales revenue as it comes in. To help bring the model to life, let's add some figures, for illustration purposes only.

Figure 7.5 shows the break-even point (BEP). Perhaps the most important single calculation in the whole costing exercise is to find the point at which real profits start to be made.

The point where the sales revenue line crosses the total costs line is the break-even point. It is only after that point has been reached that a business can start to make a profit. We can work this out by drawing a graph, such as the example in Figure 7.5, or by using a simple formula. The advantage of

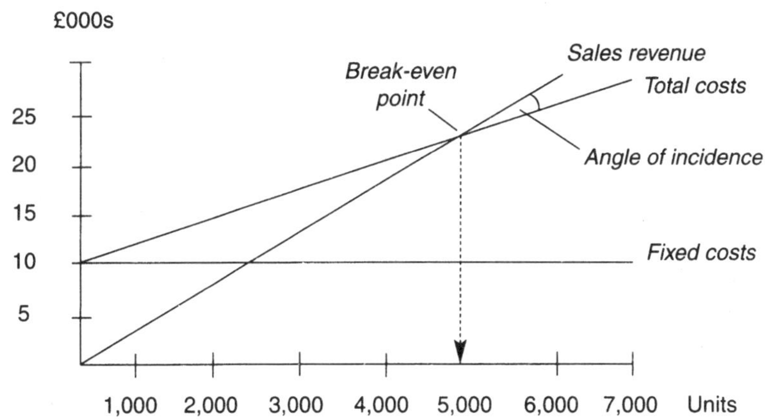

Figure 7.5 Cost model showing a break-even point

using the formula as well is that you can experiment by changing the values of some of the elements in the model quickly.

The equation for the BEP is:

$$\text{BEP} = \frac{\text{Fixed costs}}{\text{Unit selling price} - \text{Variable costs per unit}}$$

This is quite logical. Before you can reach profits you must pay for the variable costs. This is done by deducting those costs from the unit selling price. What is left (usually called the unit contribution) is available to meet the fixed costs. Once enough units have been sold to meet these fixed costs, the BEP has been reached.

Let's try the sum out, given the following information shown on the break-even chart:

Fixed costs	=	£10,000
Selling price	=	£5 per unit
Variable cost	=	£3 per unit

$$\text{So BEP} = \frac{\pounds 10{,}000}{\pounds 5 - \pounds 3} = \frac{\pounds 10{,}000}{\pounds 2} = 5{,}000 \text{ units}$$

Now we can see that 5,000 units must be sold at £5 each before we can start to make a profit. We can also see that if 7,000 is our maximum output we have only 2,000 units available to make our required profit target.

Obviously, the more units we have available for sale (ie the maximum output that can realistically be sold) after our break-even point, the better. The relationship between total sales and the break-even point is called the margin of safety.

Margin of safety

This is usually expressed as a percentage and can be calculated as shown in Table 7.1.

Clearly, the lower this percentage, the lower the business's capacity for generating profits. A low margin of safety might signal the need to rethink fixed costs, selling price or the maximum output of the business.

Table 7.1 The calculation of a margin of safety

	£	
Total sales	35,000	(7,000 units × £5 selling price)
Minus break-even point	25,000	(5,000 units × £5 selling price)
Margin of safety	10,000	
Margin of safety as a percentage of sales	29%	(10,000 ÷ 35,000)

The angle formed at the BEP between the sales revenue line and the total costs line is called the angle of incidence. The size of the angle shows the rate at which profit is made after the break-even point. A large angle means a high rate of profit per unit sold after the BEP.

Costing to meet profit objectives

By adding in the final element, desired profits, we can have a comprehensive model to help us with costing and pricing decisions.

Supposing in the previous example we knew that we had to make £10,000 profits to achieve a satisfactory return on the capital invested in the business, we could amend our BEP formula to take account of this objective:

$$\text{BEPP (break-even profit point)} = \frac{\text{Fixed costs + Profit objective}}{\text{Unit selling price} - \text{Variable costs per unit}}$$

Putting some figures from our last example into this equation, and choosing £10,000 as our profit objective, we can see how it works.

Unfortunately, without further investment in fixed costs, the maximum output in our example is only 7,000 units, so unless we change something the profit objective will not be met.

$$\text{BEPP} = \frac{\pounds 10{,}000 + \pounds 10{,}000}{\pounds 5 - \pounds 3} = \frac{20{,}000}{2} = 10{,}000 \text{ units}$$

The great strength of this model is that each element can be changed in turn, on an experimental basis, to arrive at a satisfactory and achievable result.

Let us return to this example. We could start our experimenting by seeing what the selling price would have to be to meet our profit objective. In this case we leave the selling price as the unknown, but we have to decide the BEP in advance (you cannot solve a single equation with more than one unknown). It would not be unreasonable to say that we would be prepared to sell our total output to meet the profit objective.

So the equation now works out as follows:

$$7{,}000 = \frac{20{,}000}{\pounds\text{ Unit selling price} - \pounds 3}$$

Moving the unknown over to the left-hand side of the equation we get:

$$\pounds\text{ Unit selling price} = \pounds 3 + \frac{20{,}000}{7{,}000} = \pounds 3 + 2.86 = \pounds 5.86$$

We now know that with a maximum capacity of 7,000 units and a profit objective of £10,000, we have to sell at £5.86 per unit. Now if the market will stand that price, then this is a satisfactory result. If it will not, then we are back to experimenting with the other variables. We must find ways of decreasing the fixed or variable costs, or increasing the output of the plant, by an amount sufficient to meet our profit objective.

Costing for special orders

Every small business is laid open to the temptation of taking a particularly big order at a 'cut-throat' price. However attractive the proposition may look at first glance, certain conditions must be met before the order can be safely accepted.

Let us look at an example – a slight variation on the last one. Your company has a maximum output of 10,000 units, without any major investment in fixed costs. At present you are just not prepared to invest more money until the business has proved itself. The background information is:

Maximum output	10,000 units
Output to meet profit objective	7,000 units
Selling price	£5.86
Fixed costs	£10,000
Unit variable cost	£3.00
Profitability objective	£10,000

The break-even chart will look like Figure 7.6.

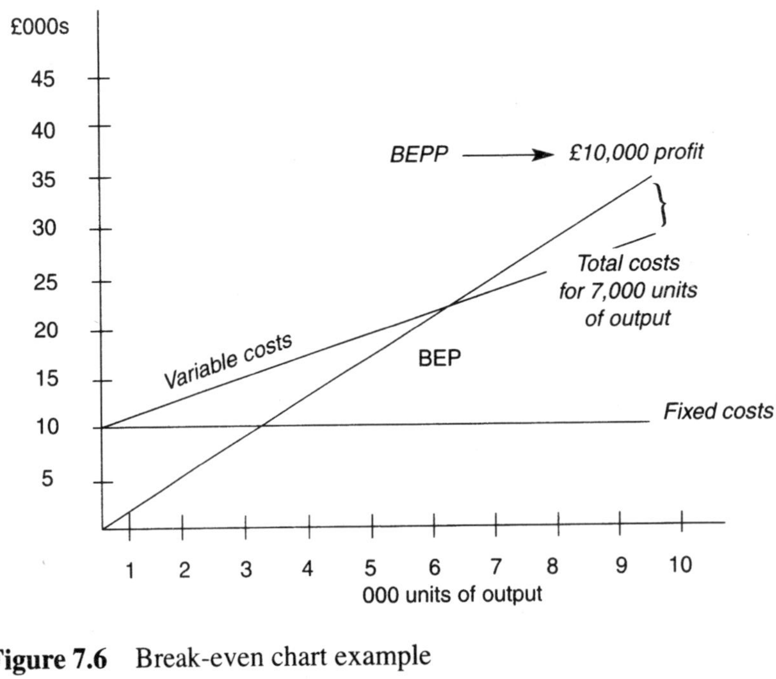

Figure 7.6 Break-even chart example

You are fairly confident that you can sell 7,000 units at £5.86 each, but that still leaves 3,000 units unsold – should you decide to produce them. Out of the blue an enquiry comes in for about 3,000 units, but you are given a strong hint that nothing less than a 33 per cent discount will clinch the deal. What should you do?

Using the costing information assembled so far, you can show the present breakdown of costs and arrive at your selling price.

Unit cost breakdown

	£	
Variable costs	3.00	
Contribution to fixed costs	1.43	(£10,000 fixed costs ÷ 7,000 units)
Contribution to meet profitability objective	1.43	(£10,000 profitability objective ÷ 7,000 units)
Selling price	5.86	

As all fixed costs are met on the 7,000 units sold (or to be sold), the remaining units can be sold at a price that covers both variable costs and the profitability contribution, so you can negotiate at the same level of profitability, down to £4.43, just under 25 per cent off the current selling price. However, any selling price above the £3.00 variable cost will generate extra profits, but these sales will be at the expense of your profit margin. A lower profit margin in itself is not necessarily a bad thing if it results in a higher return on capital employed, but first you must do the sums (see Chapter 6).

There is a great danger with negotiating orders at marginal costs, as these costs are called, in that you do not achieve your break-even point soon enough and the deal results in a loss. (Look back to the first example in this chapter to see how missed sales targets affect profitability.)

Real-time internet pricing strategies

With the advent of the internet, a new type of 'special order' has been created. With accurate information on market demand, it is possible to vary prices infinitely to meet current demand exactly.

The stock market, for example, works by gathering information on supply and demand. If more people want to buy a share than to sell it, the price goes up until the amount of supply and demand are matched. If the information is perfect (when every buyer and seller knows what is going on), the price is optimised. For most businesses this is not a practical proposition. Their customers expect the same price every time for the same product or service. In any case, customers have no accurate idea what the demand is at any given moment in time.

For the internet company, computer networks have made it possible to see how much consumer demand exists for a given product at any time. Anyone with a point-of-sale till could do the same, but the report may not come in until weeks later. This means that online companies could alter their prices hundreds of times a day, changing according to different circumstances or different markets, and so improve profits dramatically. easyJet.com, a budget airline operating in Luton, does just this. It prices to fill its planes – you could pay anything from £30 to £200 for the same trip, depending on the demand for that flight.

However, alongside real-time pricing must come real-time break-even analyses. Unless you always know your position in relation to your break-even point, it is difficult to be certain that extra sales at lower prices will result in a greater profit.

Costing for business start-up

Paradoxically, one of the main reasons small businesses fail in the early stages is that too much start-up capital is used to buy fixed assets. While clearly some equipment is essential at the start, other purchases could be postponed. This may mean that 'desirable' and labour-saving devices have to be borrowed or hired for a specific period. Obviously this is not as nice as having them to hand all the time, but if, for example, computers, fax machines, photocopiers, scanners and even delivery vans are brought into the business, they become part of the fixed costs. The higher the fixed-cost plateau, the longer it usually takes to reach the break-even point and then profitability. And time is not usually on the side of the new small business. It has to become profitable relatively quickly or it will simply run out of money and die.

Look at these two hypothetical new small businesses. They are both making and selling identical products at the same price, £10. They plan to sell 10,000 units each in the first year. The owner of Company A plans to get fully equipped at the start. His fixed costs will be £40,000, double that of Company B. This is largely because, as well as his own car, he has bought such things as a delivery van, new equipment and a photocopier. Much of this will not be fully used for some time, but will save some money now. This extra expenditure will result in a lower unit variable cost than Company B can achieve, a typical capital intensive result (see Figure 7.7). Company B's owner, on the other hand, proposes to start up on a shoestring. Only £20,000 will go into fixed costs, but, of course, her unit variable cost will be higher, at £4.50. The variable cost is higher because, for example, she has to pay an outside carrier to deliver, while A uses his own van and pays only for petrol.

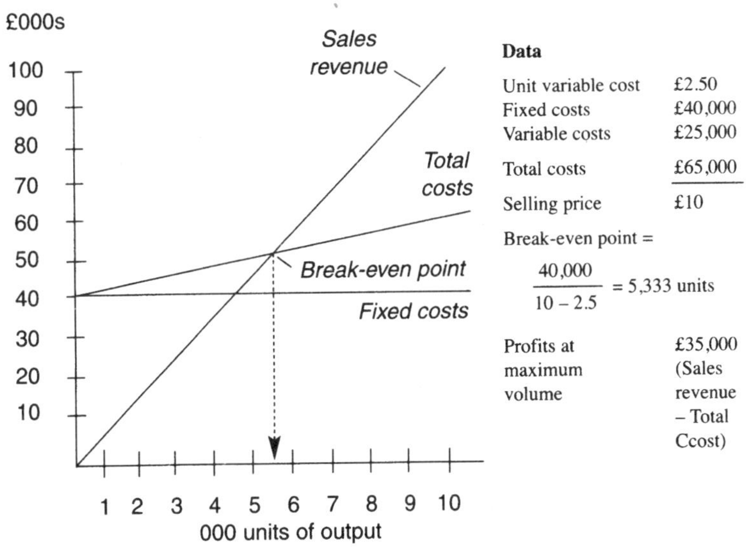

Figure 7.7 Break-even chart for Company A

The break-even chart for Company B is shown in Figure 7.8. From the data on each company you can see that total costs for 10,000 units are the same, so total possible profits, if 10,000 units are sold, are also the same. The key difference is that Company B starts making a profit after 3,636 units have been sold. Company A has to wait until 5,333 units have been sold.

Now another pair of reasons why small businesses fail very early on are connected with the marketplace. They are frequently over-optimistic on how much they can sell. They also underestimate how long it takes for sales to build up. So for these reasons, and spending too much start-up capital on fixed assets, great care should be taken to keep start-up fixed costs to the minimum.*

* There are all sorts of 'persuasive' arguments to go for a capital-intensive cost structure. In periods of high growth, the greater margin on sales will produce a higher return on capital invested (ROCE), but high fixed costs will *always* expose a new or small business to higher risks. A small business has enough risks to face, with a survival rate of less than 20 per cent in its first few years, without adding to them.

Costing to identify unprofitable products and services

Not all the business's products will always be profitable. Settling down to allocate 'real' fixed costs to products can be something of an eye-opener to owner-managers. Look at the example below. The business manufactures three

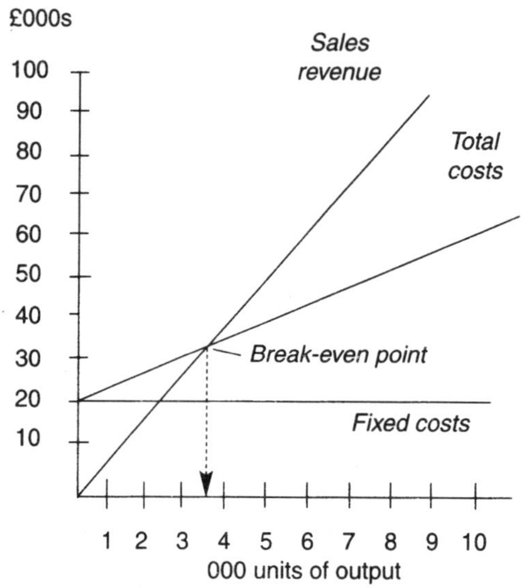

Data

Unit variable cost	£4.50
Fixed costs	£20,000
Variable costs	£45,000
Total costs	£65,000
Selling price	£10

Break-even point =

$$\frac{20{,}000}{10 - 4.5} = 3{,}636 \text{ units}$$

Profits at maximum volume	£35,000

Figure 7.8 Break-even chart for Company B

products. Product C is bulky, complicated and a comparatively slow seller. It uses all the same sorts of equipment, storage space and sales effort as products A and B, only more so. When fixed costs are allocated across the range, it draws the greatest share (Table 7.2).

This proves something of a shock. Product C is losing money, so it has to be eliminated, which will produce the situation shown in Table 7.3.

Fixed costs will not change, so the £25,000 has to be re-allocated across the remaining two products. This will result in profits dropping from £15,000 to £5,000; therefore our conventional product costing system has given the wrong signals. We have lost all the 'contribution' that Product C made to fixed costs, and any product that makes a contribution will increase overall profits. Because fixed costs cannot be ignored, it makes more sense to monitor contribution levels and to allocate costs in proportion to them.

Table 7.2 Product profitability 1

	A	*B*	*C*	*Total*
	£	£	£	£
Sales	30,000	50,000	20,000	100,000
Variable costs	20,000	30,000	10,000	60,000
Allocated fixed costs	4,500	9,000	11,500	25,000
Total costs	24,500	39,000	21,500	85,000
Operating profit	5,500	11,000	(1,500)	15,000

Table 7.3 Product profitability 2

	A	*B*	*Total*
	£	£	£
Sales	30,000	50,000	80,000
Variable costs	20,000	30,000	50,000
New allocated fixed costs	8,333	16,667	25,000
Total costs	28,333	46,667	75,000
Operating profit	1,667	3,333	5,000

Table 7.4 Allocating fixed costs by contribution level

		Contribution		*Fixed cost allocated*
		£	%	£
Product	A	10,000	25	6,250
	B	20,000	50	12,500
	C	10,000	25	6,250
Total		40,000	100	25,000

Table 7.5 Marginal costing product profit-and-loss account

	A £	%	*B* £	%	*C* £	%	*Total* £
Sales	30,000		50,000		20,000		100,000
Marginal costs	20,000		30,000		10,000		60,000
Contribution	10,000	33	20,000	40	10,000	50	40,000
Fixed costs	6,250		12,500		6,250		25,000
Product profit	3,750	13	7,500	15	3,750	19	15,000

Looking back to Table 7.2, we can see that the products made the following contributions (Contribution = Sales – Variable costs) shown in Table 7.4.

Now we can recast the product profit-and-loss account using this marginal costing basis (Table 7.5).

Not only should we not eliminate Product C, but because in contribution terms it is our most profitable product, we should probably try to sell more.

Getting help with break-even

You have a few options to get help with making break-even calculations. Your accountant can show you, and if your algebra is a bit rusty you can take a quick refresher at the BBC's Bitesize site (www.bbc.co.uk/schools/gcsebitesize/maths).

Alternatively there are a number of online spreadsheets and tutorials that will take you through the process. Biz/ed (www.bized.co.uk > Virtual worlds > Virtual learning arcade > Break-even analysis) is a simulation that lets you see the effect of changing variables on a fairly complex break-even calculation. There is SCORE (www.score.org > Business tools > Template gallery > Break even analysis). BizPep (www.bizpeponline.com/PricingBreakeven.html) sell a software program that calculates your break-even for prices plus or minus 50 per cent of your proposed selling price. You can tweak costs to see how to optimise your selling price and so hit your profit goal.

8

Improving performance

Any action that tends to increase profits whilst either not increasing or actually reducing the resources employed to generate those profits produces healthy growth. Using the summarized financial statements for High Note shown in Table 8.1, the example used in earlier chapters, we can see the effect of various growth strategies. If we can increase sales say by £10,000, whilst maintaining the profit margin at 11.21 per cent, we will have grown profits by £1,121. So both sales and profits will have grown by 17 per cent. If that can also be done without needing any more working space or money tied up in stocks, so much the better. Our return on capital will also improve.

Contrast that with, say, a strategy that grows sales, whilst costs rise disproportionately and more assets are employed to achieve that growth, then an unhealthy growth pattern will emerge.

Areas of poor or declining financial performance identified whilst monitoring performance against budget may be improved by taking one or more of a number of actions. The most fruitful places to look for better results are the prices, costs and capital employed in the day-to-day running of the business.

Pricing for profit

Small firms are often guilty of getting their prices wrong at first. The misconception that new and small firms can undercut established competitors is usually based on ignorance of either the true costs of a product or service, or of the true value of overheads.

The overhead argument usually runs like this: 'The competition is big, has plush offices, and lots of overpaid marketing executives spending the

Table 8.1 High Note's profit-and-loss account and balance sheet

Profit-and-loss account	£	**Balance sheet**	£	£
Sales	60,000	**Fixed assets**		
Less the cost of goods to be sold (materials, labour, etc)	30,000	Garage conversion, etc		11,500
		Computer		1,000
Gross profit	30,000	Total fixed assets		12,500
Less operating expenses (rent, utilities, admin, etc)	21,300			
Operating profit	8,700	**Working capital**		
Less interest due to bank	600	Current assets		
Profit before tax	8,100	Stock	9,108	
Less tax	1,377	Debtors	12,000	
Profit after tax (11.21%)	6,723	Cash	0	
			21,108	
		Less Current liabilities		
		Overdraft	4,908	
		Creditors	0	
			4,908	
		Working capital (CA – CL)		16,200
		Total assets		28,700

company's money on expense-account lunches, and I don't have any of these. Ergo, I *must* be able to undercut them.' The errors within this type of argument are, first, that the plush office, far from being an unnecessary overhead, is actually a fast-appreciating asset, perhaps even generating more profit than the company's main products (shops, restaurants, and hotels typically fit into this category). The plush office can also contribute to creating an image for the product or service in such a way that enhances its price – Harley Street consultants, for example, fit into this category. Second, the marketing executives may be paid more than you pay and may have expense accounts, but if they do not deliver a constant stream of new products and new strategies to justify the money spent, they will be replaced with people who can.

Clearly, you have to take account of what your competitors charge, but remember: price is the easiest element of the marketing mix for an established company to vary. The competition could copy your lower prices, forcing you into a price war and possible bankruptcy, far more easily than you could capture their customers with lower prices.

While most small firms – 80 per cent according to some reports – set their price with reference to costs either using a cost-plus formula (for example, the cost of materials plus 50 per cent) or a cost-multiplier formula (for example, three times materials costs), all *customers* buy with reference to *value*. That can leave a lot of scope for managing your prices up.

Price is the element of the marketing mix that is likely to have the greatest impact on the profitability of small businesses. It is often more profitable for a new company to sell fewer items at a higher price whilst getting its organisation and product offerings sorted out; the key is to concentrate on obtaining good margins, often with a range of prices and quality.

Using High Note (Table 3.2) as our working model, assume its £60,000 of sales come from 60 customers all buying £1,000 worth of goods and services from us, at 50 per cent gross profit margin. If by raising our prices by 10 per cent we lost no customers, then our profit would rise by £6,000, all of which would drop to the bottom line, before tax, as there are no additional costs involved, almost doubling our profit before tax. But what would happen if we lost six customers (10 per cent) as a result of the price rise? Now we would have only 54 customers paying £1,100 each, or £59,400. That's only £600 less than before, and there are other benefits that have not been shown.

The above sums depend on your level of gross profit. The lower your gross profit, the less business you can afford to lose for any given price rise. Download a spreadsheet that does all the arithmetic of changing prices for you from Innovator.com (www.innovator.com > Free business plan templates and financial plan models > Free break even model and pricing tools – full version).

Reducing costs

Costs are associated with activity. But, as activity is often allocated wrongly, it follows that the opportunity for cost reduction is almost always greater than you think.

This is demonstrated by the 80/20 rule – the Pareto principle. You can test this principle by looking at your own business. A close examination of your client list will show that 20 per cent of them account for the vast majority of your business and perhaps all of your profit. Yet you spend as much time servicing unprofitable customers as you do profitable ones.

What makes cost reduction so powerful is the disproportionate effect on profits that even a small reduction in costs can have. Look at Table 8.2; you can see that for a business making a 5 per cent net profit, reducing costs by just 2 per cent will raise profits by 40 per cent from £50,000 to £70,000. The company may well have needed to find 10 per cent or even 20 per cent more customers to have the same effect on the only place that matters: the bottom line.

Table 8.2 Cost savings matter

	Before		*After 2% cost saving*		*Extra performance*	
	£000s	*%*	*£000s*	*%*	*£000s*	*%*
Sales	1,000	100	1,000	100	–	–
Costs	950	95	930	93	–20	–2
Profit	50	5	70	7	+20	+40

Some other ways to reduce costs

- Acquiring customers is an expensive process; they have to be found, wooed and won. Once you have them onside they cost less to keep, spend more money with you and are less price-sensitive than new customers. Retaining them will do more than almost any other marketing strategy to lower marketing costs and so grow your profit margin. According to research carried out by Bain (www.bain.com > Consulting expertise > Capabilities > Customer strategy & marketing > Customer loyalty), a 5 per cent increase in customer retention can improve profitability by 75 per cent.
- Improve your buying, for example by joining an online buying group such as Buying Groups (www.buyinggroups.co.uk), Power Purchasing

Group (www.ppg.co.uk) or e-Three (www.e-three.com) that helps buyers to join forces and by buying in bulk get better prices and terms of trade.

- Change product and/or service mix, which can be done if you sell more than one product or service or are planning to introduce new ones as part of your growth strategy. Analyse costs so that energies are focused on those with the highest profit margin. Very few managers have any true idea as to which products or services generate the most profit, so collecting the data has to be the first step (see Chapter 7).

Squeezing working capital

Once you have bought your shop, set up your factory or bought your delivery vehicle, they are 'sunk' costs. You may want more, but you are limited by the amount of capital. However, you do have discretion over your working capital; the more you squeeze it, the less money you have tied up in the business for a given level of activity. That, in turn, means lower borrowing costs.

The evidence points to small firms being inefficient users of working capital. The smaller they are, the less efficient they tend to be (see Figure 8.1).

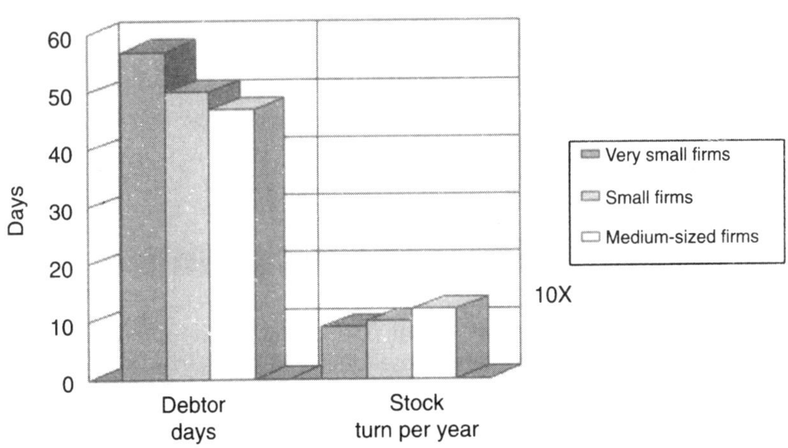

Figure 8.1 Very small firms can have poor control of working capital

Here are some things you can do to make better use of your working capital:

- Find out when your biggest customers have their monthly cheque run and make sure your bills reach them in time.
- Send out statements promptly to chase up late payers and always follow up with a phone call.
- Always take trade references when giving credit and look at the client's accounts to see how sound they are.
- Have accurate stock records and monitor slow-moving stock.
- Have an accurate sales-forecasting system (a sound budgeting process will do) so you can match stock and work according to likely demand.
- Take credit from your suppliers up to the maximum time allowed. Try and negotiate extended terms with major suppliers once you have a good track record. Many will say no, but some may not. The advent of a price rise is a good moment to begin negotiating.
- Make any cash you have work harder. Use overnight money markets via an internet bank to get interest on cash rather than having it sitting in the banking system earning you nothing.
- Work out whether it makes sense to pay bills quickly to take advantage of early-settlement discounts. Sometimes – usually by accident – suppliers offer what amounts to high rates of interest for settling up promptly. If you are offered 2½ per cent to pay up now rather than in two months time, that is equivalent to an annual rate of interest of 15 per cent (12/2 × 2½ per cent). If your bank is charging you 8 per cent, then you will make a good extra profit by taking up this offer.
- Bank cheques and cash promptly. It's not only safer, but the sooner you get money into the banking system, the sooner you are either saving interest cost or earning interest income.

The profit-improvement programme

Once you have completed your review of past performance and identified the areas for improvement, you need to prepare an action plan to show exactly how all this hidden profit is to be released.

Set improvement targets for each area, as shown in the Figure 8.2. The tasks identified as needed to achieve these results should be incorporated into your next budget review. Where an opportunity to improve is substantial and the work involved is minimal, 'seize the hour' and start improving profits straight away.

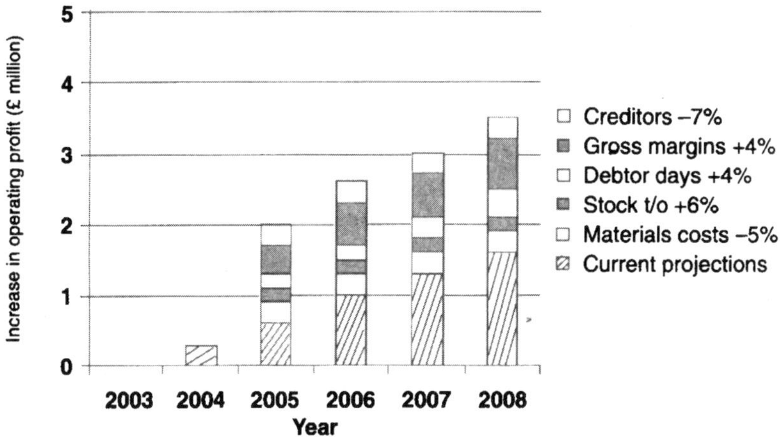

Figure 8.2 Releasing hidden profitability

3

Figuring out the future

9

Revenue budgets

Everyone has made a budget or plan at some time. In our personal lives we are always trying to match the scarce resource 'pay' with the ever-expanding range of necessities and luxuries in the marketplace, a battle we all too often lose, with mortgage costs, car running expenses, food and children's clothes taking more cash out than we can put in. Usually the domestic budget is confined to a periodic attempt to list and total likely future bills. These are then split into essential and non-essential items. The 'essential' total is then deducted from expected pay (or income) and if anything is left over we can plan how to spend it.

Temporary shortages of cash are made up by taking out an overdraft, the judicious use of a credit card, or talking to a rich aunt.

Every year we review how well we have kept within our budget and moan about the unexpected expenses that always knock us off course. The usual result is that next year's pay rise just about clears the overdraft in time to start again.

Budgeting for a business

A business has to do much the same type of budgeting and planning, although much more thoroughly if it wants to survive and prosper. A business's environment is much more complex than an individual's. For example, most people have only one main source of income, and the amount of money they are likely to get in any one year is fairly easy to predict accurately. Even the smallest business has dozens or even hundreds of potential sources of income – customers – but forecasting how much they will spend is not so easy. Some small businesses start off with their plans in the owner's head or on the back of the proverbial envelope. Most of these end up going broke in the first year. (There are simply not enough 'rich aunts' to go round.)

The central problem is that to make a profit a business must take risks. A new small business must take many more risks than an established or larger one, with each risk having more important consequences if things go wrong. For example, an established firm with a thousand customers can 'afford' to lose a few customers to the competition. A firm with a dozen customers cannot afford to lose any.

There is no way to eliminate all risks in business. Successful entrepreneurialism is all about anticipating the sort of risks that have to be taken, and understanding how they will affect the business. This knowledge is then used as the basis of a plan or budget. Putting this information together usually means gathering facts and opinions on the marketplace, interpreting their probable impact on your business, deciding what you want to happen, and finally deciding how you intend to make things happen; in other words, developing your strategy.

The small business that starts its life with a well-thought-through plan has great advantages over the 'seat of the pants' type of business. For a start, the plan or budget acts as a means of communicating your intentions to three vitally important audiences: the entrepreneur, the staff and the providers of finance. It is the entrepreneur's own 'dry run' before real money is put into the business and possibly lost. He or she can experiment with various sales levels, profit margins and growth rates to arrive at a realistic picture of how he or she would like the business to develop, before committing himself to a particular course of action. We looked at a variation of this approach in Chapter 7 when we examined the relationship between cost/volume/profit and prices. This process will give the entrepreneur an invaluable insight into the mechanics of the business and help him or her to prepare for problems before they happen.

Also, other people working in the business will be in a better position to pull together if they know where the business is going. They can then become committed to common goals and strategies.

Bankers or shareholders outside the business will be more likely to be supportive if they see that the owner-manager knows what he or she wants to happen, and how to make it come about. For example, they will not be surprised by calls for cash to finance sales growth, or capital expenditure if they have seen the plans in advance.

Finally, most people who start up in business are fairly competitive. The budget acts as a standard against which they can measure their own business performance. This is particularly important for a new business in its first trading period, with no history to go on. In other words you cannot really try to do better than last year if there wasn't one, so the only guide available is a realistic and achievable plan.

Timescale and detail

Any attempt at planning invariably begs the question 'How far ahead should I plan?' The answer 'As far ahead as you can usefully see' is not particularly helpful, but it is the one most frequently given. Here are a few guidelines that may help bring the planning horizon into view.

Outsiders, such as bankers, may have a standard period over which they expect you to plan, if you want to borrow money from them. Usually this is at least three years, and for a new business preparing its first plan, three years is probably at the horizon itself.

The *payback period*, discussed in Chapter 10, is another useful concept. If it is going to take you four or five years to recover your original investment and make a satisfactory profit, then that is how far you may want to plan.

The *rate of technological* change is yet another yardstick used in deciding how far ahead to plan. If your business is high-tech or substantially influenced by changes in technology, then that factor must influence your choice of planning horizon. Companies in the early stages of the computer business who looked only three years ahead would have missed all the crucial technological trends, and as technological trends are vital factors influencing the success of any business in this field, the planning time horizon must accommodate them.

The amount of detail with which you plan may also help to make a long planning horizon more feasible. For example, every business should plan its first year in considerable detail. As well as a description of what the business is going to do, these plans should be summarized into a month-by-month cash-flow projection;* a comprehensive quarterly profit-and-loss account; and a full opening and closing position balance sheet. This first-year plan is usually called the *budget.*

Future years could be planned in rather less detail, giving only quarterly cash-flow projection, for example. If the planning horizon is very long, plans for the final years could be confined to statements about market (and technological) trends, anticipated market share and profit margins. The detail of these plans is covered more comprehensively later in this chapter.

*In a cash business such as a shop you need to project cash flow on a weekly basis.

One final point before we look at how the budget and plans are prepared. There is a tendency to think of the budgeting process as a purely financial exercise, rather theoretical and remote from the day-to-day activity of the business. This is a serious misconception, usually fostered in larger companies, where the planners and the doers lead separate existences. People who have spent time in a large organisation have to recognise that in a small business the decision maker has to prepare his or her own planning. No one likes to have someone else's plans foisted upon him or her, a useful point to remember if a small business has a number of decision takers working in it.

In the end the budgets and plans are expressed in financial terms: cash-flow forecasts, profit-and-loss accounts and balance sheets. But the process of preparing the budget is firmly rooted in the real business world.

Objectives

'To the man who does not know where he is going – any road will take him there.' Every plan needs to start with a clear objective if it is to succeed. At the simplest level, for example, imagine you are planning a journey. Before you can consider whether to fly, drive, walk or take a train, you have to know your destination. You also have to know when you want to arrive and how much baggage you need with you. In other words, a clear objective. 'I want to be in Edinburgh on Thursday not later than 11 am with no more than an overnight bag.' This is a clear, unambiguous objective and only now can you plan the route and the means of transport in the most effective manner.

A business also needs clear objectives to be stated before the budgeting and planning process can get under way. It needs both market and financial objectives to cover the range of its activities.

Market objectives

Sometimes referred to as the business mission or purpose, market objectives go beyond a simple statement of what product(s) you are going to sell. This mission should define precisely the market you are entering and in a way that helps you to understand the needs you are trying to satisfy. To some extent products come and go, but markets go on forever – at least the needs that the products aim to satisfy do. A simple reflection on the way in which people satisfy the need to travel will illustrate the transient nature of products. While the need to travel has grown rapidly over the past 50 years, with more people travelling more often, 'products' such as the railways and ocean liners have declined. New 'products', the motor car, the coach and the aeroplane have absorbed all the extra demand and more. (It goes without saying that this market must be compatible with your own skills and resources. A fundamental mismatch in this area would be fatal.)

For example, you may be skilled at designing and making clothes. The marketplace could be vast. You could concentrate on high fashion, one-off dresses, perhaps produce a range of inexpensive clothes for young girls, or you could make and market baby clothes. Each of these markets is different, and until you define your 'mission' you cannot start to plan. The following statement is the mission of one small business: 'We will design, make and market clothes for mothers-to-be that make them feel they can still be fashionably dressed'. This meets the two criteria every mission must meet.

First, it is narrow enough to give direction and guidance to everyone in the business. This concentration is the key to business success, because it is only by focusing on specific needs that a small business can differentiate itself from its larger competitors. Nothing kills off new business faster than trying to do too many different things too quickly. But the mission narrows down the task in clear steps: we are concentrating on women; this is further reduced to women at a certain stage in their lives, ie pregnancy; this is finally reduced to those pregnant women who are fashion conscious. This is a clearly recognized need which specific products can be produced to satisfy. This is also a well-defined market that we can come to grips with.

Second, the example mission opens up a large market to allow the business to grow and realize its potential.

Interestingly enough, one of the highest incidences of failure in small businesses is in the building trade. The very nature of this field seems to mitigate against being able to concentrate on any specific type of work, or customer need. One successful new small builder defined his mission in the following sentence. 'We are going to concentrate on domestic house repair and renovation work, and as well as doing a good job we will meet the customer's two key needs: a quotation that is accurate and starting and completion dates that are met.' When told this mission, most small builders laugh. They say it cannot be done, but then most go broke.

At the end of the day, there has to be something unique about your business idea or yourself that makes people want to buy from you. That uniqueness may be confined to the fact that you are the only photocopying shop in the area, but that is enough to make you stand out (provided of course that the area has potential customers).

Also, within the market objective area you need some idea of how big you want the business to be. Your share of the market, in other words. It certainly is not easy to forecast sales, especially before you have even started trading, but if you do not set a goal at the start and you just wait and see how things develop, then one of two problems will occur. Either you will not sell enough to cover your fixed costs and you will lose money and perhaps go out of business. Or you will sell too much and run out of cash, ie overtrade (see Chapter 2).

Obviously, before you can set a market share and sales objective you need to know the size of your market. We shall consider how to find that out in the next section of this chapter. Later on, when the business has been trading for a few years, it may be possible to use that sales history and experience to forecast ahead. If there are few customers, then you can build up likely sales on a customer-by-customer basis. If there are many, then some simple mathematical technique, perhaps computer based, could be used.

But to a large extent the 'size' you want your business to be is more a judgement than a forecast, a judgement tempered by the resources you have available to achieve those objectives and, of course, some idea of what is reasonable and achievable and what is not. You will find the range of discretion over a size objective seriously constrained by the financial objectives chosen.

Profit objectives

The profit objective of every business must be to make a satisfactory return on the capital employed. We saw in Chapter 6 that, unless the return on capital employed ratio was at a certain level, a business would find it very difficult to attract outside funds. A bank manager would be fairly cool to a request for a long-term loan well below market rates. By definition 'market rates' means he or she could lend the money elsewhere at a satisfactory rate.

Another yardstick might be how much profit other people make in this type of business, even how much you could make if you invested elsewhere.

As well as making a satisfactory ROCE, the business and its profits have to grow, otherwise it will not earn enough to replace equipment or launch new products, both costly exercises. And without working equipment and a fresh product range to match the competition a business is effectively dead or dying.

So the main objectives of a new business with, say, £50,000 start-up capital, that wanted to double sales in four years, grow a little faster than the market, make a healthy and growing ROCE, and increase slightly its profit margin, might be summarised as follows:

Table 9.1 Business objectives

	Start-up budget	*Planning period*	*4 years on*
Sales	£80,000	Details	£160,000
Profit margin	12.5%	omitted	13.5%
Profit	£10,000		£21,600
Capital employed	£50,000		£86,400
ROCE	20%		25%
Market share	5%		7%

Without a well-defined mission and clearly stated objectives a business leaves its success to chance and improvisation. (Chance leads most small businesses to fail in their first three years.)

Once we have set these primary objectives, the purpose of the budget and plans is to make sure we can achieve them. Stating the objectives provides a clear guide to future action. For example, it is obvious from the primary objectives on ROCE and profit margins that an extra £36,400 (£86,400 – £50,000) of capital is needed to finance the desired sales growth over the period of the plan.

There is a school of thought that says you have to build up your plans from an appreciation of markets and resource, as described below. Then an objective can be deduced as the sum of the achievable tasks. But this exposes you to the question 'What if this sum is not satisfactory?' It could also leave opportunity untapped. Neither of these is a very satisfactory position, so the objective's first approach, and then market appreciation, must be adopted.

Market appreciation

All businesses live or die by virtue of their success or otherwise in the marketplace. People very often talk of a particular market or business sector as being profitable, but without much idea of why. Years of research into the factors that influence a market's relative profitability have produced the following conclusion. 'The more intense the competition, the lower the return on capital employed.' While that does not come as a great surprise in itself, it does provide some valuable pointers on how to analyse the marketplace. It follows that any budget or plan must be based on a sound appreciation of the competitive forces at work in a market, otherwise the primary profit objective may simply not be attainable.

For someone who has not yet started up a business, this process can act as a filter to eliminate the undesirable. For those already trading, it can provide guidance on areas upon which to concentrate and on likely problem areas.

Figure 9.1 shows a way to look at these competitive forces as a whole.

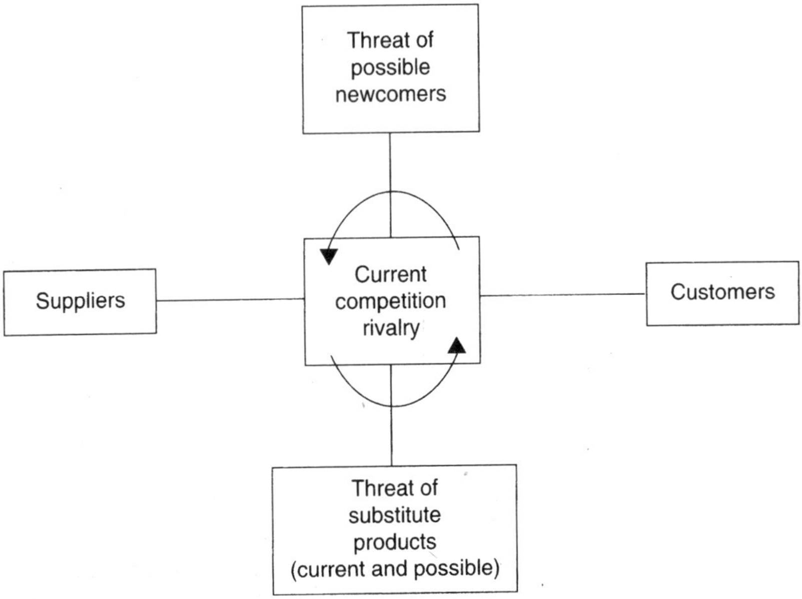

Figure 9.1 Competitive forces in a market

Before you can start to plan in any detail you need answers to the following questions:

- *Where is my market?* The starting point in any market appreciation has to be a definition of the scope of the market you are aiming for. A small general shop may only serve the needs of a few dozen streets. A specialist restaurant may have to call on a catchment area of 10 or 20 miles. While trends and behaviour in the wider market are helpful facts to know, your main activity is within your own area.

  You may eventually decide to sell to several different markets. For example, a retail business can serve a local area through its shop and a national area by mail order. A small manufacturing business can branch out into exporting. People all too often flounder in their market research by describing their markets too broadly; for example, the motor industry, when they really mean car sales in Perth, or health foods, when they mean wholemeal bread in one small village.

- *Who are the customers, potential and actual?* Some products are aimed at the general public, others at particular trades or professions, males or females only, or perhaps large institutions and government departments. Some products cut across all these customer groups.

  Focusing on the particular people who could buy the product gives a better idea of how many are likely to buy. Equally important, it will help you understand why they should buy from you. This really is the key to the whole business and its growth.

  One entrepreneur started up a drinks vending machine business. Finding a vending machine that was reliable and easy to operate and maintain was the first task he tackled. This took two months. Next he searched for suitable ingredients, ending up with a very acceptable and economic range of hot and cold drinks. He then found a finance company to lease machines to his customers. All this vital background work took nearly four months and eventually he hit the road selling. He quickly found that his potential customers were new or smallish businesses without a vending machine already, most of which were unacceptable to the leasing company because they had no financial track record. Or he had to find a large company that was on the point of changing its equipment for one reason or another. The nature of his potential customers meant he had to call cold. (An advertising campaign using leaflets would take a long time to produce sales and he had already spent half his working capital.) He had to make something like 80 cold calls to get two interviews and it took 10 interviews to get three quotations in. Only one of those would result in an order. He ran out of cash before he could get a significant number of customers, as well as having a nervous breakdown from cold calling, a task he did not enjoy. Bringing his potential customers sharply into focus at the start and taking account of them in his business plan might have avoided this disaster.
- *How big is the market?* You need to know this to see whether or not your sales objectives are reasonable and attainable. If there are only 1,000 possible customers for your product in the geographical market you have chosen, and five well-established competitors, then expecting to sell to 500 of them in year 1 is not on.
- *Is the market growing or contracting?* In a growth market there are often opportunities for new companies to come in, or for small businesses to expand. In a contracting market existing competitors slog it out, leaving little room for new entrants or expansion. You should find out in which

direction the market is moving and at what speed. The state of the general economy may not have much bearing on the market you are in. For example, the number of video rental outlets reached their zenith in a period of economic decline in the United Kingdom.

- *Who are the competition and what are their strengths and weaknesses?* Most products have competitors. To some extent this is reassuring because you know in advance that you are likely to achieve some sales, but you have to identify who they are and how they can affect your business. You have to know everything about them: their product range, prices, discount structure, delivery arrangements, specifications, minimum order quantities, terms of trade, etc.

  You also have to look at two less visible types of competitor. First, those who have not yet arrived on the scene. You have to consider what conditions would attract new businesses into the market. For example, businesses that require very little start-up capital, or add little value to goods, are always vulnerable to new competitors opening up. On the other hand, a business that can protect its ideas with patents, or achieve high-volume sales quickly, is less exposed. Second, under certain circumstances customers can be persuaded to buy a quite different or substitute product from the one you are offering, and still satisfy their same needs. In other words, you have a secondary layer of competition.
- *Who are the suppliers?* Most businesses buy in and process raw materials of one sort or another. They add value, sell out, and make a profit. If you have only a handful of possible suppliers, then they have the initiative and can set the terms of trade. For a new small business the problem is very often one of finding someone to supply in small enough volume. Nevertheless, it is a key strategic task to find at least two sources of supply for all vital products, and to negotiate the best possible deal. Otherwise the products themselves will be uncompetitive.

Forecasting sales

One of our primary market objectives is how much we would like to sell – or need to sell to achieve profit objectives. For a new business this and market share may be the only guidelines as to what sales volume could be achieved. The new business could also see what other similar ventures had achieved in their early years. However, a business with a sales history has another clue – the sales trend.

Figure 9.2 shows the quarterly sales results of a hypothetical business that has been trading for the past two years. Sales have grown from about 50 units per quarter up to just over 200 in the eight quarters.

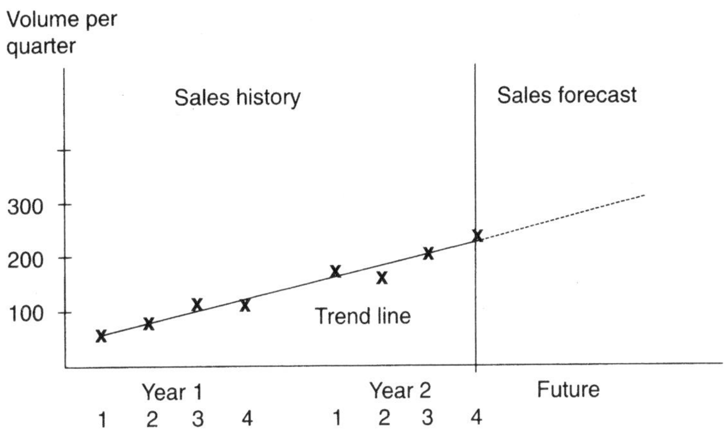

Figure 9.2 Graph showing sales trend

It is possible, either mathematically or by eye, to fit a trend line through these points. Continuing this trend line over the planning period shows what sales are likely to be, if the past can be accepted as a good guide to the future.

Now we can superimpose our sales objective on to a chart showing the sales trend. This will show the gap between where the business is going by virtue of its own momentum, and where we should like sales to be (see Figure 9.3).

Apart from continuing our present efforts to achieve sales and sales growth, our objectives call for extra results to fill the sales gap, so within our sales operating plan specific tasks to achieve this growth have to be identified.

It is beyond the scope of this book to give more than an outline of the task involved in a market appreciation suitable for preparing a business plan. While most financial matters are common to all types of enterprise, most marketing matters are unique to a particular business.

On the SCORE website (www.score.org > Business tools > Template gallery > Sales forecast) there is a downloadable Excel spreadsheet from which you can plan future sales and compare performance with that of previous years. Once you are satisfied with your sales projection, use the profit-and-loss projection (www.score.org > Business tools > Template gallery > Profit and loss projection (3 years)) to complete your budget.

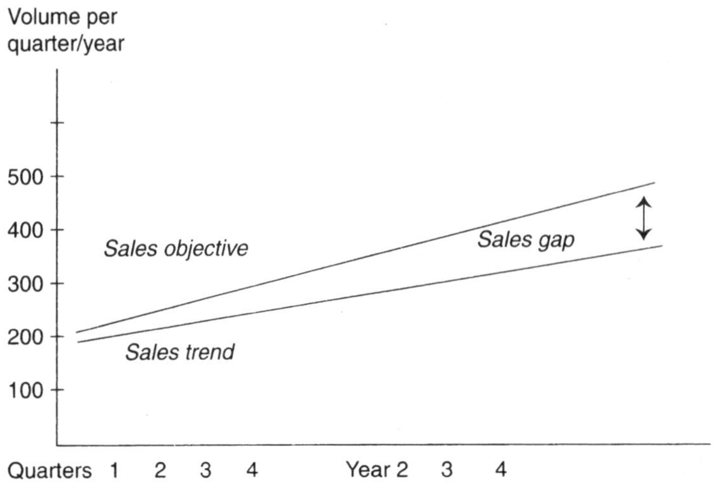

Figure 9.3 Gap analysis

Resources appreciation

Market appreciation is a look outside the business to see the opportunities and threats to the business and its products. A business reacts to these by mobilising its resources to take advantage of the opportunities and to neutralise the threats. Business resources can be loosely grouped under four main headings: people, facilities, information and finance.

People audit

People are vital to the success or failure of the business. Before you begin to identify specific people it is probably more important to highlight the sorts of skills and knowledge you want them to have. So the process could be summarised as a series of questions with the answers giving some guidance for future action.

Auditing your own knowledge and skills is an obvious starting point. By identifying gaps in these you can decide whom you need. The worksheet on page 121 will help to get ideas flowing.

You can then search out other people or agencies that you need to help achieve your objectives.

Figure 9.4 Personal skills resource audit

How good are you at:

	Satisfactory	*Inadequate*	*Person/ help available*	*If not, what will you do?*
MARKETING				
Market research				
Salesmanship				
Publicity/advertising				
Product development				
Distribution				
Others (list)				
PRODUCTION				
Technical matters				
Buying				
Planning production				
Quality control				
Stock control				
Others (list)				
PEOPLE				
Selecting people				
Leading people				
Motivating people				
Teamwork				
Listening to people				
Giving clear instructions				
Others (list)				
FINANCE AND ADMINISTRATION				
Forming a company or partnership				
Finding premises				
Bookkeeping, tax and VAT				
Raising money				
Budgeting and managing money				
Collecting in money				
Writing letters				
Forward planning				
Dealing with regulations				
Others (list)				

Facilities audit

Facilities, such as an office, workshop space, storage, machinery, etc, are another key resource. The worksheet below can summarise the position here.

1. What fixtures, fittings, premises, etc do you have or need? List.

Need	*Have*	*Can borrow*	*Must find*

2. What production equipment, etc do you have or need? List.

Need (including some idea of output that can be achieved	*Have*	*Can borrow*	*Must find*

3. Other key facilities.

You may find you already have resources you do not need. You should either put them to use or dispose of them if they cannot be pressed into service soon. They will only increase the fixed-asset base of the business, tie up capital unnecessarily and make it harder to achieve your ROCE objective. (Look back at Chapter 5 to refresh your memory.)

Information audit

Information, other than pure market information, is also an important and frequently neglected resource area. Carry out an information audit.

1. What bookkeeping system have you planned? Who will run it and will it give you the control you need?
2. Are there any possible legal problems related to:
   - your product or service;
   - your premises;
   - present or future employees;
   - yourself (ie conditions in a past service contract may prevent you from working in a certain field);
   - patents, etc?

Financial resources audit

Financial resources are clearly an important consideration in any planning process. They are nearly always the major constraint in any plans for a new business, whether starting up or expanding. A financial resources audit looks for answers to three questions. How much money have you got that you are prepared to commit to your business? How much do you need? Where will you get the balance from?

1. Obviously the first thing to do is to find out exactly how much you have to invest in the business. You may not have much in ready cash, but you may have valuable assets that can be converted into cash, or other borrowing. The difference between your assets and liabilities is your 'net worth'. This is the maximum security that you can offer for any money borrowed, and it is to be hoped that the calculations in Table 9.2 will yield a pleasant surprise.

Table 9.2 Your net worth

Liabilities	£	*Assets*	£
Overdraft		Cash in hand and in banks, building societies, National Savings or other deposits	
Mortgage		Stocks and shares	
Other loans		Current redemption value of insurance policies	
Hire purchase		Value of home	
Tax due, including Capital Gains		Any other property	
Credit cards due		Motor car(s), etc	
Garage, local shop accounts due		Jewellery, paintings and other marketable valuables	
Any other financial obligations	________	Any money due to you	
		Value of your existing business	________
Total liabilities	________	Total assets	________

Net worth = Total assets – Total liabilities

2. The sum you need to achieve your plan is calculated as follows:
   (a) First-year start-up costs: £
   Fixed capital (tools, equipment, premises, etc)
   Working capital (materials, opening stocks, wages, rent, your living expenses, etc)
   ____
   Total start-up costs
   ____
   (b) Additional capital to finance growth. (In Table 9.1, the additional capital required is £36,400.)
   (c) Total capital required over planning period is the total of (a) and (b).
3. The capital you need to find is the amount by which 2 exceeds 1.

Key strategies and operating plans

So far in the budgeting and planning process we have set our business objectives, looked at market opportunities and examined our own resources. The next step is to decide what resources to commit to what market and business tasks.

Key strategies are areas of action that are vital to the success of the business. The market strategies define exactly what products/services you plan to offer to which specific customer group(s). The financial strategies explain the sources of funds and the profitability expected.

An *operating plan* must be made for each area of the business. For example, sales, advertising, production, equipment purchasing, raw material supplies, premises, deliveries, etc. The operating plan must state the specific task to be achieved and when; what will be done, by whom, and by what date. It should also monitor results. If appropriate, each task should also have an expense budget estimate against it. Your plans are complete when you have set enough tasks to achieve your primary business objectives. These plans must not be complicated, but they must be written down. They provide the backbone to the business, and the statement for others (bankers, shareholders, etc) to see that you know your business direction.

An example of an operating plan is shown in Table 9.3.

People launching a small business or trying to expand never cease to be amazed at how long their plans take to come to fruition. The much quoted rule is to estimate a timescale, double it, then double it again for good measure. The problem is that most of them simply do not think through their plans step by step, in the manner prescribed for an operating plan. Small businesses simply do not have the cash resources to allow for extensive timescales.

Contingency plans

Any plan is built on a number of assumptions. Many of these assumptions are outside the planner's control, and some are keys to the success of the venture. Look back at the earlier example of a personal objective to get to Edinburgh by a certain time (page 112). Suppose, after reviewing all the market opportunities (ie trains, planes, hire cars, buses, etc) and assessing our resources (ie money, our own car, etc), we decide to go by train. Unfortunately, when we get to the station we find the train has been cancelled.

Table 9.3 Example of an operating plan

Operating plan, year _______

Planning area	Task/objective budget	Cost	Timescale	Action required	Date	By whom	Results of task on costs
Premises	Find 2,000 sq ft of warehouse space within five miles of workshop	£800	April–July (must be in and working by 1 August)	1. Look at area.	6/5	GFK	
				2. Contact estate agents a, b, c.	6/5	GFK	
				3. Search papers.	10/5	GFK	
				4. Visit possible sites.	10/6	GFK	
				5. Review leases.	20/6	TRD	
				6. Sign up.	1/7	TRD	
				7. Take over premises.	20/7	GFK	
Raw material suppliers	Find two competitive suppliers of raw material 'x'	Petty cash	April–June	1. Search trade journals.	6/5	TJ	
				2. Write for specification and quotes.	10/5	TJ	
				3. Chase up replies.	15/5	TJ	
				4. Visit four best possibles.	20/5	TJ	
				5. Place trial orders.	25/5	TRD	
				6. Select two best.	15/6	TRD	
				7. Place orders.	25/6	TJ	

A key assumption in our plan is that the train will run – but this is clearly outside our control. If by going for the train, we miss the opportunity to fly, and it is then too late to go by car or bus, we have no contingency plans – no means of achieving our objective. Now obviously in this example we could postpone going to Edinburgh, or perhaps arrive later after telephoning to explain.

But there are business situations where our objectives must be met on time, and viable contingency plans have to be prepared to make sure this happens.

For example, if a piece of production equipment breaks down, do you know where you can hire or borrow a spare quickly? Small businesses cannot afford to be out of commission for long, so contingency arrangements for all sensitive areas are essential.

Setting the budget

Only now is it possible to construct a detailed financial picture of a business's budget and plans. The budget sets out, line by line in much the same format as the profit-and-loss account, the major sources of income and expenditure for the period of the budget. The year is broken down into weeks or months, depending on the dynamics of the business.

The best way to budget is to look one year ahead and review the whole budget each quarter. At that review, add a further quarter to the forecast so that you always have a one-year budget horizon. This is known as a 'rolling quarterly budget'. It may seem like hard work at first, but the sooner budgeting becomes a regular business routine rather than an annual chore, the more accurate your forecasts will become. This not only makes the whole planning process both easier and more reliable, but it can also have the knock-on effect of making your business more creditworthy and valuable. Any business that consistently meets or exceeds its targets will have its profit targets accepted more readily than one with a patchy performance in relation to its targets.

Budget guidelines

- The budget must be based on realistic but challenging goals. Those goals are arrived at by both a top-down 'aspiration' and a bottom-up forecast of what seems both possible and likely. For example, if sales have been growing at a rate of 10 per cent a year for the past couple of years, a 10 per cent increase in sales seems a 'possible and likely' outcome for next year – a target that your sales force might be expected to aim for. However, your business plan may involve an attempt to grow at a faster rate than in the past. In this case, a goal of 15 per cent would be acceptable – challenging, but realistic.

- The budget should be prepared by those responsible for delivering the results – the salespeople should prepare the sales budget and the production people the production budget. You need to manage the communication process so that everyone knows what other parties are planning for.
- Agreement to the budget should be explicit. During the budgeting process, several versions of a particular budget should be discussed. For example, the boss may want a sales figure of £2 million, but the sales team's initial forecast is for £1.75 million. After some debate, £1.9 million may be the figure agreed upon. Once a figure is agreed, a virtual contract exists that declares a commitment from employees to achieve the target and commitments from the employer to be satisfied with the target and to supply resources in order to achieve it. It makes sense for this contract to be in writing.
- The budget needs to be finalized at least a month before the start of the year and not weeks or months into the year. The sooner people know their goals, the sooner they can start to achieve them.
- The budget should undergo fundamental reviews periodically throughout the year to make sure all the basic assumptions that underpin it still hold good. For example, the market itself may be growing much faster than you expected, so rendering your goals too easy to achieve.
- You need up-to-date and accurate information to make the process worthwhile. Figures should be ready for review 7 to 10 working days before the month's end.

Monitoring performance

Performance needs to be carefully monitored and compared against the budget as the year proceeds, and corrective action must be taken where necessary to keep the two consistent. This has to be done on a monthly basis (or using shorter time intervals if required), showing both the company's performance during the month in question and throughout the year so far.

Looking at Table 9.4, we can see at a glance that the business is behind on sales for this month, but ahead on the yearly target. The convention is to put all unfavourable variations in brackets. Hence, a higher-than-budgeted sales figure

Table 9.4 The fixed budget

Heading	*Month*			*Year to date*		
	Budget	*Actual*	*Variance*	*Budget*	*Actual*	*Variance*
Sales	805*	753	(52)	6,358	7,314	956
Materials	627	567	60	4,942	5,704	(762)
Materials margin	178	186	8	1,416	1,610	194
Direct costs	74	79	(5)	595	689	(94)
Gross profit	104	107	3	820	921	101
Percentage	**12.92**	**14.21**	**1.29**	**12.90**	**12.60**	**(0.30)**

* Figures indicate thousands of pounds

does not have brackets, while a higher materials cost does. We can also see that, while profit is running ahead of budget, the profit margin is slightly behind (–0.30 per cent). This is partly because other direct costs, such as labour and distribution in this example, are running well ahead of budget.

Flexing the budget

A budget is based on a particular set of sales goals, few of which are likely to be exactly met in practice.

Table 9.4 shows a company that has used £762,000 more materials than budgeted. As more has been sold, this is hardly surprising. The way to manage this situation is to flex the budget to show what, given the sales that actually occurred, would be expected to happen to expenses. This is done by applying the budget ratios to the actual data. For example, materials were planned to be 22.11 per cent of sales in the budget. By applying that to the actual month's sales, a materials cost of £587,000 is arrived at.

Looking at the flexed budget in Table 9.5, we can see that the company has spent £19,000 more than expected on the material given the level of sales actually achieved, rather than the £762,000 overspend shown in the fixed budget.

Table 9.5 The flexed budget

Heading	*Month*			*Year to date*		
	Budget	*Actual*	*Variance*	*Budget*	*Actual*	*Variance*
Sales	753*	753	–	7,314	7,314	–
Materials	587	567	20	5,685	5,704	(19)
Materials margin	166	186	20	1,629	1,610	(19)
Direct costs	69	79	(10)	685	689	(4)
Gross profit	97	107	10	944	921	(23)
Percentage	**12.92**	**14.21**	**1.29**	**12.90**	**12.60**	**(0.30)**

* Figures indicate thousands of pounds

The same principle holds for other direct costs, which appear to be running £94,000 over budget for the year. When we take into account the extra sales shown in the flexed budget, we can see that the company has actually spent £4,000 over budget on direct costs. While this is serious, it is not as serious as the fixed budget suggests.

The flexed budget allows you to concentrate your efforts on dealing with true variances in performance.

Seasonality and trends

The figures shown for each period of the budget are not the same. For example, a sales budget of £1.2 million for the year does not translate to £100,000 a month. The exact figure depends on two factors. The projected trend may forecast that, while sales at the start of the year are £80,000 a month, they will change to £120,000 a month by the end of the year. The average would be £100,000.

By virtue of seasonal factors, each month may also be adjusted up or down from the underlying trend. You could expect the sales of heating oil, for example, to peak in the autumn and tail off in the late spring. Figure 9.5 suggests what this might look like when displayed on a chart.

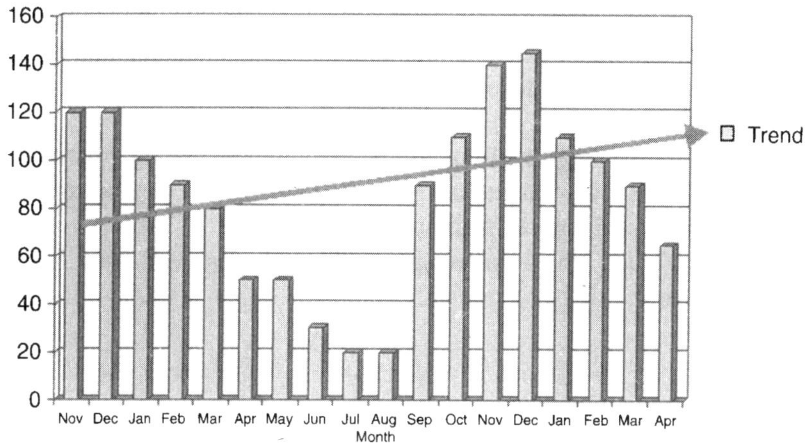

Figure 9.5 Seasonal budget showing trend

Cash and capital budgets

The budget will not just have implications on profit and loss. If sales goals are high, there may be a requirement for more equipment to produce the product. This would have capital implications as more funds may have to found.

Also, there may be implications on cash flow. Rapidly increasing the number of sales of manufactured products necessitates spending large amounts of cash on raw materials and labour, and financing debtors until they pay up. As long as sales growth accelerates, spending increases. This is not necessarily harmful, but it must be budgeted for by preparing a cash-flow forecast based on the budget.

Building a budget model

Setting a budget requires discussion with key staff – several different sets of figures may have to be produced. A budget model built using a spreadsheet is the ideal way to compile these. By using spreadsheets, the effect on the budget of changing any figure or figures can be seen automatically and instantly without any tedious calculations. All that is required is for someone to decide the relationship between the various elements of the budget – for example, that debtors will be given 45 days to pay, or that the gross margin should be 50 per cent. Thereafter, changes in sales levels as the budget is formulated will just 'roll down' the model to produce revised profit-and-loss accounts and balance sheets.

A further advantage of going for a computerised bookkeeping system is that it has a budgeting model framework built in. The model is also useful for budget updates and revisions throughout the year.

See Chapter 10 for free business planning tools that will help with the budgeting process.

10

Capital budgets

Most businesses discover quite early on that the equipment, machinery, space, etc that they started up with is not adequate for their future needs. That does not necessarily make the owners bad businesspeople; it just shows how difficult it is to predict the future shape of any business. Perhaps they prudently chose second-hand items, or they were extremely conservative in their sales forecasts, and now simply cannot meet the demand. In any event decisions have to be taken on new investments. Should existing equipment be replaced? Should more space be acquired?

If the answer to both these questions is yes, then decisions have to be made on which equipment or space should be chosen.

It is very rare that one piece of equipment is the only absolutely correct one for the job. Suppliers compete, and most products have significant differences. They may cost more but last longer, or cost less but be more expensive to run.

Work space in offices and shops also comes in different shapes, sizes and locations. All these capital decisions have two things in common. They usually involve (a) spending or committing a lump sum *now* to get (b) a stream of benefits in the future.

Anyone buying a new piece of equipment expects it to be used to help make more products that will in turn produce cash and profits. The same argument is true if equipment is being replaced. The equipment that produces the best return should be chosen. But how will it be chosen? What tools are available to help make a sound financial choice?

Clearly it is important to try to get these decisions right. After all, these types of assets tend to be around for a long time. Also, their resale value declines rapidly in the early years. Anyone who has bought a new car will not need further emphasis on this point.

Average return on capital employed (ARCE)

We know that one of the two primary objectives of a business is to make a satisfactory return on the capital employed in the business. Clearly, any new capital investment will have to achieve that same objective.

Until now we have only looked at the return on capital employed for an individual year. This would not be enough to see if a new investment proposal was worthwhile. Imagine your own reaction if someone asked you for £1,000 and explained how they could return only £200 at the end of the first year. You would expect them to come up with a complete proposal, one that covered the return of all the money you had lent – plus interest.

The same is true of any capital investment proposal. We have 'lent' the project, whatever it may be, a sum of capital. We expect a return on that capital over the working life of the assets bought. The ARCE method sets out to do just that. It measures the average profit over the life of a project and compares that with the capital employed.

Let us take an example to illustrate the method. A company is considering buying a new lathe for £5,000. The working life of the lathe will be five years, by which time it will be worthless. Net profit from the output of the lathe will come in as shown in Table 10.1.

Table 10.1 The ARCE method

	Year		*Net profit (after charging 100% depreciation)* £
	1		500
	2		1,000
	3		2,000
	4		2,000
	5		175
Total	5	years	5,675

Over the five years the capital invested in the lathe will produce an average return of £1,135 (5,675 ÷ 5) each year. As the capital concerned is £5,000 and the average return is £1,135, then the average return on the capital employed is 22.7 per cent or (1,135 ÷ 5,000) × 100.

This figure is simple to calculate and is of some help. For example, if on average the business buying the lathe is making a return of 30 per cent on capital employed, then buying the lathe will dilute the ROCE of the business as a whole.

Table 10.2 shows what happens to ROCE when the present business and the new project are 'merged' together to form the new business.

Table 10.2 Limitations of ARCE 1

Present business	+	*New project*	=	*New business*
	£	£		£
Average net profit	6,000	1,135		7,135
Capital employed	20,000	5,000		25,000
ROCE	30%	22.7%		28.5%

While this information is of some use as a tool for helping with capital investment decisions generally, ARCE has two severe limitations.

Let us suppose that the company has decided to buy a lathe – but there are two on offer. The first we have already examined. Profits from this lathe will build up gradually over the years and tail off sharply in the final year. The second lathe has rather different characteristics. It swings into action immediately, achieves high profits and tails off over the last three years (see Table 10.3).

Table 10.3 Limitations of ARCE 2

	Year	*Net profit from 2nd lathe (after charging 100 per cent depreciation)*	*1st lathe net profit*
		£	£
	1	2,650	500
	2	2,650	1,000
	3	125	2,000
	4	125	2,000
	5	125	175
Totals	5 years	5,675	5,675

As the overall total profits are the same, over the five years this investment will also produce an ARCE of 22.7 per cent. And yet, if all other factors were equal and only the figures on these pages had to be considered, most businesspeople would prefer the second lathe project. The reason they would give is that they get their profit in quicker. By the end of the second year that lathe would have paid for itself, while the first would not 'break even' until well into year 4.

This would be a 'gut reaction' and it would probably be right. That does not mean that gut reactions are better than financial techniques; it just means we have got the wrong technique. We need a technique that takes account of when the money comes in – clearly timing matters.

This leads into average rate of return's other major failing. It uses profit as one of the measures, although a business may have to wait months or even years for that profit to be realized as cash.

The other measure it uses is the cash spent on a capital investment, so like is not being compared with like: profit on the top of the equation and cash on the bottom. Two projects could generate identical profits, but if one generated those profits in immediate cash, the ARCE technique would not recognize it. But a businessperson's 'gut reaction' would once again choose the project that brought in the cash the soonest. And once again it'd be right.

Payback period

A more popular technique for evaluating capital investment decisions is the payback period method.

Payback attempts to overcome the fundamental weaknesses of the ARCE method. It compares the cash cost of the initial investment with the annual cash net inflows (or savings) that are generated by the investment. This goes beyond simply calculating profit as shown in the profit-and-loss account, which is governed by the realization concept. The timing of the cash movements is calculated. That is, for example, when debtors will actually pay up, and when suppliers will have to be paid. By using cash in both elements it is comparing like with like.

Payback also attempts to deal with the timing issue by measuring the time taken for the initial cost to be recovered.

Table 10.4 illustrates the method.

The payment period is three years. That is when the £10,000 initial cash cost has been matched by the annual net cash inflows of £2,000, £4,000 and £4,000 of the first three years. Now we have a method that uses cash and takes some account of time.

Table 10.4 The payback method

	£
Initial cost of project	10,000
Annual net cash inflows	
Year 1	2,000
2	4,000
3	4,000
4	2,000
5	1,000

Unfortunately it leaves us with a result that is difficult to compare directly with the profit performance of the rest of the business. If the business is currently making a 25 per cent return on capital employed, and a project has a payback period of three years, will the project enhance or reduce overall profitability? Without further calculation this question cannot be answered – and even then the answer will not necessarily be correct. Look again at the preceding example. The payback method looks only at the period taken to repay the initial investment. The following years are completely ignored, and yet the net cash inflows in those years are a benefit to the business, and their size matters.

This weakness is brought sharply into focus when competing projects are being compared.

Let us suppose your task is to choose between Projects A and B purely on financial criteria (see Table 10.5).

The payback period for each proposal is three years, which signals that each project is equally acceptable on financial grounds. Clearly this is nonsense. It seems highly probable that Project B, which generates an extra £6,000 cash, is a better bet.

Payback has some merits, not least of which is its simplicity. It is often used as a cut-off criterion in the first stages of an evaluation. In other words, a business decides that it will not look at any project with a payback period greater than, say, four years. This provides a common starting point from which a more exacting comparison can be made. Beyond that use, the method's weaknesses make it a poor tool to use in investment decisions in a small business.

Big businesses do not expect to get all their capital investment decisions right. Small businesses have to, as their very survival depends on it.

Table 10.5 Limitations of payback

	Project A £	*Project B* £
Initial cost of project	10,000	10,000
Annual net cash inflows		
Year 1	2,000	2,000
2	4,000	4,000
3	4,000	4,000
4	500	4,000
5	250	2,000
6	250	1,000
Total cash in flow	11,000	17,000
Payback period	3 years	3 years

Discounted cash flow

Neither the ARCE nor the payback method for evaluating capital investment projects is wholly satisfactory. They provide neither a sound technique for deciding whether or not to invest, nor a technique to help choose between competing projects. They fail for the reasons already described, but they also fail for a more fundamental reason.

The businessperson's gut feeling that timing is important is perhaps more true than he or she thinks. No one is going to invest a pound today, unless he or she expects to get back more than a pound at some future date. The level of that reward, if you like, is related in some way to the riskiness of the investment. But whatever the level of risk, no one wants less money back as that would involve making a loss.

The factor that alters the value of an investment over time is the interest rate. The longer the time period or the higher the interest rate, the larger is the final sum returned. This relationship between the initial sum invested and the sum finally returned is familarly known as compound interest.

The *compound interest equation* that calculates the precise figure for any interest rate or time period is:

$$\text{Future value} = £P \times (1 + r)^n$$

In this equation P = the initial sum invested, or principle, r = the interest rate expressed in decimals, and n = the time period in years.

So if we invest £100 for three years at 10 per cent we can expect a future value of:

$$
\begin{aligned}
& £100 \times (1 + 0.1)^3 \\
= & £100 \times (1.1)^3 \\
= & £100 \times (1.1 \times 1.1 \times 1.1) \\
= & £100 \times 1.331 \\
= & £133.10
\end{aligned}
$$

For the doubters, the sum can be worked out in longhand (Table 10.6).

Table 10.6 Compound interest calculation

	Start	*Year 1*	*Year 2*	*Years 3*
	£	£	£	£
Balance brought forward	100.00	100.00	110.00	121.00
Interest at 10%		10.00	11.00	12.10
Value of investment	100.00	110.00	121.00	133.10
				~~Finish~~

You could consider the situation to be similar to looking through a telescope: looking forward in time through the compound interest equation magnifies the value of an investment.

But what happens when you look through the other end of a telescope? Images appear to shrink. To some extent this is similar to the problem a businessman might face when making up his mind about capital investment decisions. He knows he is not prepared to pay £1 now to get £1 back in the future; that would be bad business. What he has to calculate is exactly how much less than £1 he would pay to receive £1 back in, say, one year's time.

The thinking might go something like this. 'For this kind of investment I have to make 10 per cent profit, so I need to know what figure less 10 per cent will equal £1, and that is what I will pay now.' This is rather like moving to the other end of the telescope and looking backwards.

This problem is exactly the inverse of compounding and is called discounting. To calculate the appropriate discount factor we simply stand the compound interest equation on its head.

Discounting calculations

$$\frac{1}{(1+r)^n} = \frac{1}{(1+0.1)^1} = \frac{1}{1.1} = 0.909$$

So we would recommend that only £0.909 is paid today for £1 to be received in a year's time.

You can test the equation yourself by adding 10 per cent to £0.909. It should total £1.00.

Now we have an equation that lets us allow for the time value of money. (This is nothing whatever to do with the effects of inflation. Those effects are important and are covered later in this chapter.) Let us look at the ways to put the concept to use.

Present value

Just as the future value of an investment can be calculated using compounding, so the present value of cash coming in during the years ahead can be calculated using discounting.

We have already seen the heart of the present value equation. In full, using the same symbols as for compound interest, it is:

Present value equation

$$\text{Present value} = £P \times \frac{1}{(1+r)^n}$$

The basic requirement of any present-value calculation is that you have some idea of what percentage profit you want from an investment. That is not usually a very difficult problem. If you have to borrow the money at 12 per cent, pay tax on the profits and take risks as well, it is not too hard to focus on an acceptable range of interest rates.

Alternatively, the yardsticks of current returns, competitors' or industry returns, or even a personal objective, can all be used to help arrive at an acceptable cut-off interest rate for discounting. Below this cut-off rate, a project is simply not acceptable.

Look at the following example. The proposition is that you should invest £50,000 now to make £80,000 over the next five years: a clear profit of

Table 10.7 Example showing the cash flow of investment

Year	*Cash out*	*Cash in*	*Net cash flow*
	£	£	£
0	50,000	–	(50,000)
1	5,000	15,000	10,000
2	5,000	15,000	10,000
3	12,500	37,500	25,000
4	12,500	37,500	25,000
5	5,000	15,000	10,000
			30,000

£30,000, apparently a satisfactory situation. The cash will come in and out as shown in Table 10.7.

This is based on a £50,000 investment now, followed by some cash expenses and cash income in the future. In other words, a typical business buying in materials, adding value and selling mainly on monthly terms. The fourth column shows the net cash flow for each year of the project's life. Cash in exceeds cash out by £30,000 – in other words the profit.

However, we know that the net cash flow received in future years is not worth as much as present pounds. Remember, no businessperson will pay £1 now to receive only £1 back in the future. Our problem is to discount all the future cash flows back to present values.

Once again we could use our present value equation, but that would be rather time consuming. Fortunately there are tables that do all the sums for us, and this facility is becoming increasingly available on calculators.

Table 10.8 shows the present value discount factor over five years for a rate of 17 per cent. You can see the factors and the effect of time on money value at the website www.bplans.com/common/calculators/dcf.cfm. There you have both the numbers and a neat chart showing the decay in value.

All we have to decide on now is a discount rate. Well, if we know we can have a risk-free investment of 12 per cent, it may not seem worthwhile taking a risk unless we can make 17 per cent, a modest enough figure for a risk project.

Using the discount tables we can select the appropriate year and interest rate, to arrive at the present value factor (Table 10.8).

Take the present value factor for each year and multiply it by the net cash flow. This gives the net present value of the cash that this investment generates. In this case it comes to £49,370 (8,550 + 7,310 + 15,600 + 13,350 + 4,560),

Table 10.8 Example showing the present value of cash flow of investment

Year	*Net cash flow*	*Present value factor at 17%*	*Net present value*
	£		£
0	(50,000)	1.000	(50,000)
1	10,000	0.855	8,550
2	10,000	0.731	7,310
3	25,000	0.624	15,600
4	25,000	0.534	13,350
5	10,000	0.456	4,560
			(630)

which is £630 less than the £50,000 we put in. So if you had expected to make a 17 per cent return on your investment, you would have been disappointed.

Interestingly enough both the ARCE and payback methods would probably have encouraged you to go ahead. ARCE would have come up with average profits of £16,000 per annum, which represents a 32 per cent return on capital employed, and the payback period is 3 years and 2½ months – not long at all. But the fatal flaw in both these methods is revealed clearly by the present value concept. The timing of the cash flow over the working life of the investment is crucial, and that must form the central part of any judgement on whether or not to invest.

The profitability index

Present value is clearly a superior capital investment appraisal method, overcoming the weaknesses of the other two techniques. But in its present form it only provides the answer to our first question. Should we invest or not? Having decided on the level of return (interest) we want, and calculated the net cash flow, we simply discount to arrive at the net present value. If this is greater than zero, then the project is acceptable.

Suppose, like our problem with the lathes, the question is not simply whether or not to invest, but also to choose between alternatives, then would the present value method work? The fairly extreme example in Table 10.9 will highlight the difficulty of using the present value method alone to solve both types of problem.

Here we have two possible projects to invest in. One calls for capital of £7,646 and the other for £95,720. Leaving aside the problem of finding the

Table 10.9 Comparing projects using the present value method

	Project A			Project B		
Year	*Net cash flow*	*Present value factor at 10%*	*Net present value*	*Net cash flow*	*Present value factor at 10%*	*Net present value*
	£		£	£		£
0	(7,646)	1.000	(7,646)	(95,720)	1.000	(95,720)
1	3,000	0.909	2,727	30,000	0.909	27,270
2	4,000	0.826	3,304	40,000	0.826	33,040
3	5,000	0.751	3,755	50,000	0.751	37,550
		Present value	9,786		Present value	97,860
		Net present value	2,140		Net present value	2,140

money, which is the better investment proposition? If we are happy with making a 10 per cent return on our investment, then both projects are acceptable. Both end up with a net present value of £2,140, so that cannot be the deciding factor. Yet it is clear that A is a better bet than B, simply because the relationship between the size of the investment and the present value of the cash flow is 'better'.

The way these elements are related is through the profitability index, which is set out below:

The profitability index

$$\text{Profitability index} = \frac{\text{Present value of earnings}}{\text{Cost of investment}}$$

In this example the index for Project A is 128 per cent (9,786 ÷ 7,646), and for B 102 per cent (97,860 ÷ 95,720). The profitability index clearly signals that Project A is the better choice.

In fact, any comparison of projects that do not have identical initial investments and lifetimes can only be properly made using the profitability index.

To summarize then, the first step is to see if the various possible projects are acceptable by discounting their net cash flows at the cut-off interest rate. If a choice has to be made between the acceptable projects, calculate each one's profitability index, and then rank them as shown on Table 10.10.

Table 10.10 Example showing project ranking by profitability index

Project	*Profitability index* %
A	135
B	127
C	117
D	104
E	101

It is not possible to have a profitability index lower than 100 per cent. That would imply a negative net present value, which in turn would eliminate the proposal at the first stage of the evaluation process.

Internal rate of return

One important piece of information has not been provided by either the net present value or the profitability index. A capital investment proposal may have a satisfactory net present value, that is a positive one, at our cut-off interest rate. It may also come out ahead of other choices in the profitability index ranking, but we still do not know exactly what rate of return we can expect to get.

This is important information for three main reasons. First, it allows us to compare new investment proposals with the rest of the business, something that neither present value nor the profitability index will do. Second, it gives us a yardstick understood by people outside the business. For example, bankers or other potential investors will understand a proposal for funds with a straightforward percentage as the end result. They will not be so sure of a figure such as £1,000 net present value. This could be misunderstood for the total profit, and be rejected. Finally, under most circumstances, the internal rate of return, as this is known, is a satisfactory method of comparing projects. (In any doubtful situations the profitability index will be the deciding factor.)

We do know, however, that the rate of return must be greater than the cut-off interest rate, provided, of course, that the net present value is positive.

Table 10.11 shows how Project A's net present value was calculated in the profitability index example.

Table 10.11 Calculating the internal rate of return 1

Year	*Net cash flow* £	*Present value factor at 10%*	*Net present value* £
0	(7,646)	1.000	(7,646)
1	3,000	0.909	2,727
2	4,000	0.826	3,304
3	5,000	0.751	3,755
		Present value	9,786
		Net present value	2,140

We know that Project A is expected to make a rate of return higher than 10 per cent simply because the net present value is positive. If we increase the present value to, say, 20 per cent by arbitrarily raising our cut-off level, we can see whether it meets that test (Table 10.12).

Table 10.12 Calculating the internal rate of return 2

Year	*Net cash flow* £	*Present value factor at 10%*	*Net present value* £
0	(7,646)	1.000	(7,646)
1	3,000	0.833	2,499
2	4,000	0.694	2,776
3	5,000	0.579	2,895
		Present value	8,170
		Net present value	524

We can see that the project still shows a positive net present value at our new cut-off rate of 20 per cent. However, the figure is much smaller and suggests we are getting close to the 'internal rate of return'. That is the discount rate which, when applied to the net cash flow, results in a zero net present value. We could go on experimenting to reach that rate, but this would be time consuming, and not very rewarding, for reasons explained at the end of the chapter.

There is a simple technique known as interpolating, which we can use provided we have one positive and one negative net present value figure.

This is how interpolation works: let us select a discount rate that we are reasonably certain will lead to a negative net present value, for example 25 per cent (Table 10.13).

Table 10.13 Calculating the internal rate of return 3

Year	Net cash flow £	Present value factor at 25%	Net present value £
0	(7,646)	1.000	(7,646)
1	3,000	0.800	2,400
2	4,000	0.640	2,560
3	5,000	0.512	2,560
		Present value	7,520
		Net present value	(126)

Now we know that the internal rate of return must lie between 20 and 25 per cent. That is because the project had a positive net present value at 20 per cent and a negative one at 25 per cent. Using the interpolation equation we can arrive at a good approximation of the discount rate.

Interpolation equation

$$\text{Internal rate of return (IRR)} = \text{Lowest trial rate} + \left[\frac{\text{Positive cash flow}}{\text{Range of cash flow}}\right] \times \left[\frac{\text{Difference between}}{\text{high and low rates}}\right]\%$$

For this example the equation would be:

$$\text{IRR} = 20 + \left[\frac{524}{524 + 126} \times (25 - 20)\right] \%$$

$$= 20 + 4.03\% = 24.03\%^{*} = 24\%$$

*It is normal practice to use only whole numbers when calculating rates of return.

Had we used the net present value figure from the 10 per cent discount calculation, we would have arrived at a different IRR. The reason is that to give an accurate IRR figure, both net present value figures used in the interpolation equation must be fairly small.

Risk and sensitivity analysis

Discounted cash flow (DCF) gives us a sound tool for deciding whether an investment proposal is acceptable or not. It also helps us to choose between competing projects. DCF can perform one more important task: it can be used to examine the circumstances that could make a project unacceptable.

Look back at Table 10.12. If the cut-off interest rate is 20 per cent, this project is acceptable. The net cash flow has been calculated on a series of assumptions about sales levels, days' credit taken and given, expenses, etc. But what if any one of those assumptions is wrong? For example, supposing debtors pay up much more slowly and the resultant cash flow takes longer to build up – but of course lasts longer, with some people not paying up until year 4?

Table 10.14 shows how the cash flow will look if these new 'assumptions' occur.

Under these circumstances the investment would not be acceptable, so now we know how 'sensitive' the project is to customers paying up promptly. We have to assess what the risk is of these new circumstances occurring.

Table 10.14 Example of a sensitivity analysis

Year	*First estimate of net cash flow* £	*New estimate of net cash flow* £	*Present value factor at 20%*	*Net present value* £
0	(7,646)	(7,646)	1.000	(7,646)
1	3,000	2,000	0.833	1,666
2	4,000	3,000	0.694	2,082
3	5,000	4,000	0.579	2,316
4		3,000	0.482	1,446
Total positive cash flow	12,000	12,000	Present value	7,510
			Net present value	(136)

The same technique can be applied to any of the assumptions built into the cash-flow forecast, and a good, or robust, investment proposal is one that can withstand a range of 'what if...?'-type tests.

Dealing with inflation

A common assumption is that varying the discounted cash-flow cut-off point is a good way to deal with inflation. For example, if you felt that 20 per cent was a good rate of return last year, and inflation is set to be 6 per cent next year, then 26 per cent should be the new cut-off rate.

Although attractively simple, the logic is wrong. Inflation is already dealt with in the assumptions built into the cash-flow forecast (or it certainly should be). For example, the sum covering payments for materials is based on three assumptions: the volume of materials needed, how much they will cost, and when they will be paid for. The middle assumption here is where inflation is allowed for.

Appraising investments

So far we have treated DCF as though it were exclusively for looking at investments in fixed assets. Any investment in fixed assets almost inevitably has an effect on working capital levels. DCF techniques have to be able to accommodate both fixed and working capital factors in investment decisions.

Some general factors in investment decisions

Some considerable space has been devoted to the subject of new investment appraisal. It is an area where many small businesses get into fatal problems very early on. People starting up rarely have a proper framework for deciding how much money to invest in a business idea. They are usually more concerned with how to raise the money. A critical look using discounted cash flow would probably change their minds, both about how much to spend on starting up and on expansion.

However, in the end, any investment appraisal is only as good as the information that is used to build up the cash-flow forecast. Much of the benefit in using DCF is that it forces investors to think through the whole decision thoroughly.

The bulk of the work in investment appraisal is concerned with:

1. Assessing market size, market share, market growth and selling price.
2. Estimating and phasing the initial cost of the investment; working life of facilities; working capital requirements.
3. Assessing of plant output rate.
4. Ensuring that the provision of additional services and ancillaries has not been overlooked.
5. Estimating operating costs.
6. Estimating the rate of taxation.
7. Estimating the residual value of the asset.

The relatively simple task is that of using sound investment appraisal techniques.

Online capital budgeting calculator

Solutions Matrix (www.solutionmatrix.com > Download center > Download Financial Metrics Lite for Microsoft Excel) has a useful tool for working out payback, discounted cash flow, internal rate of return and a whole lot more calculations relating to capital budgeting. You have to register on the site first before downloading their free capital budgeting spreadsheet suite and tutorial.

11

Preparing a business plan

As 9 out of 10 businesses start without a business plan and over half of established businesses don't have one you could be forgiven for believing that preparing one is a luxury you can live without. Though not having one may appear to save time and money, especially if you don't have outside backers to report to, the statistics would suggest otherwise. According to research carried out at Cranfield School of Management, over 70 per cent of the fastest-growing and most successful businesses started out with a written business plan. You might, as in the case study below, survive without a business plan, but as this founder discovered he needed one anyway and would have saved a lot of pain had be started out with one.

Johnnie Boden's first catalogue was hand-drawn by a friend, with just eight items. That was back in 1991, and since then the business has come from bedroom to boardroom by way of a near-catastrophic lack of capital. The mail order company now competes with Gap, Marks & Spencer and John Lewis for a slice of the mainstream fashion market. With sales in 2007 of £129.5 million and profits of £22.75 million Boden (www.boden.co.uk) has reason to feel pleased, but it very nearly wasn't the success story it undoubtedly is. In an interview with *Real Business* (www.realbusiness.co.uk > Article) Boden explained why for the first three years the mail order clothes company was losing money hand over fist. 'We kept on running out of cash', says Boden. 'Although the concept was strong, I had no decent business plan.'

Why you need a business plan

Every business could have a less rocky formative period than Boden if it starts out with a soundly based business plan rather than ending up with one to rescue it from the brink of catastrophe. Certainly, preparing a plan can take a couple of weeks' hard work, albeit that can be spread over the months before you commit to future strategies. There are at least four compelling reasons why every business should have a current business plan:

- *It gives you confidence in the concept.* Carrying out the basic customer and competitor research that is the foundation of any business plan gives you a greater certainty that the strategy will actually work. All businesses have a number of wrinkles that can be smoothed out when preparing the business plan and at a much lower cost than by letting your customers tell you later.
- *It clarifies the scale of resources needed.* Although in his own words Boden's was not a 'swanky start-up' he did pump in £300,000 early on. With hindsight he felt the company really needed double that sum to have a decent chance of success, but as Boden started with money from a legacy left by an uncle he not unnaturally wanted to live within those means. But he was lucky; many are less so: far better to have a clear idea of how much money is really required to carry out a particular plan than to run out of cash before the strategy can prove its worth.
- *It improves your financing prospects.* As Johnny Boden inherited a legacy he was able to sidestep some of the problems of raising money. But most businesses need some outside money, even if it is only by way of a bank loan or an overdraft. And the more successful you are, the more money you need. Typically a mail order business has £1 of capital invested to generate £2 of sales, so while Boden could squeak by with £300,000 when its turnover was less than £2 million, now it needs more like £50 million.
- *It rehearses you for the future.* When a business is successful, grows and takes on more staff you will need to prepare and update business plans on a regular basis. This will be one of the primary ways of involving everyone, new and old, in your business, shaping future plans and putting them into effect. No one expects every event as recorded on a business plan to occur as predicted, but the understanding and knowledge created by the process of business planning will prepare the business for any changes that it may face and so enable you to adjust quickly.

Contents of the plan

While there is no such thing as a 'universal' business plan format, certain layouts and contents seem to have gone down better than others. These are some guidelines to producing an attractive business plan, from both an owner's and a financier's perspective.

Cover and table of contents

First, the cover should show the name of the business, the date on which the plan was prepared and your name, addresses (including e-mail), phone number and mobile number. Anyone reading the business plan may want to talk over some aspects of the proposal before arranging a meeting.

Having written the business plan you will know exactly where everything in it is, but other readers need some pointers to guide them through the maze: that's what the table of contents does. Number each main section, marketing, finance, people and so forth, 1, 2, 3; important elements within a section can then be designated 1.1, 1.2 and so on.

Executive summary

This is the most important part of your plan and will form the heart of your 'elevator pitch' (see below). Written last, this should be punchy and short – ideally one page but never more than two – and should enthuse any reader. Its primary purpose is to get an outsider, bank manager, business angel or prospective partner, to want to read the rest of the business plan and to persuade your spouse or housemates that you have a better use for the spare room than they do. It should include:

- What your product or service is, why it's better than or different from what is around now and why customers need what you plan to offer.
- How close you are to being ready to sell your product or service and what if anything remains to be done.
- Why you have the skills and expertise to start up and run this business; who else you need to help in your business; and who they are or how you will recruit them.
- Financial projections showing how much money you need to start up and operate for the first year or so; if you don't have sufficient money, how

much will you need to raise and what security can you offer to a lender or shareholding for an investor?

- How you will operate your business? Sketch out the key steps, from buying in any raw materials, through to selling, delivering and getting paid.
- Why you want to start from here rather than elsewhere, how much space you will need and for how long you believe it will be possible to run the business from this location.

You should also produce a succinct table showing past performance in key areas and future objectives, which will give readers a clear view of the scale of the task ahead (see Table 11.1).

Table 11.1 Executive summary – history and projections

Last year	*This year*	*Business area*	*Year 1*	*Year 2*	*Year 3, etc*
		Sales turnover by product/ service			
		1.			
		2. etc			
		Total sales			
		Gross profit percentage			
		Operating profit percentage			
		Total staff numbers			
		Sales staff numbers			
		Capital employed			

The contents – putting flesh on the bones

Unlike the executive summary, which is structured to reveal the essence of your business proposition, the plan itself should follow a logical sequence such as this:

- *Marketing:* with information on the product or service on offer, customers and the size of the market, competitors, and proposed pricing, promotion and selling method.
- *Operations:* with information on any processes such as manufacture, assembly, purchasing, stockholding, delivery and fulfilment, and website.

- *Financial projections:* with information on sales and cash flow for the next 12–18 months, showing how much money is needed, for what and by when.
- *Premises:* what space and equipment will be needed and how your premises will accommodate the business whilst staying within the law.
- *People:* what skills and experience you have that will help you run this business, what other people you will need and where you will find them.
- *Administrative matters:* whether you have any intellectual property (IP) on your product or service; what insurance you will need; what book-keeping and accounting system you will use; how you will keep customer, supplier and employee records.
- *Milestone timetable:* this should show the key actions you have still to take to be ready to sell your product or service and the date these will be completed.
- *Appendices:* use these for any bulky information such as market studies, competitors' leaflets, customer endorsements, technical data, patents, CVs and the like that you refer to in your business plan.

All these topics are covered in this book, and by using the index and table of contents you can find your way to them quickly.

Using business planning software

There are a number of free software packages that will help you through the process of writing your business plan. The ones listed below include some useful resources, spreadsheets and tips that may speed up the process but are not substitutes for finding out the basic facts about your market, customers and competitors:

- BizPlanit.com (www.bizplanit.com/free.html) has free resources, including free business plan information, advice, articles, links and resources, a free monthly newsletter, and the 'Virtual Business Plan' to pinpoint information.
- Bplans.com (www.bplans.com), created by Palo Alto Software, offers thousands of pages of free sample plans, planning tools and expert advice to help you start and run your business. The site has 60 free sample business plans on it, and its software package, Business Plan Pro, has these

plans plus a further 140. The sample business plans are tailored for every type of business from aircraft rental to wedding gowns.

- Royal Bank of Canada (www.royalbank.com/sme/index.html) has a wide range of useful help for entrepreneurs as well as a business plan writer package and three sample business plans.

Tips on communicating the plan

If you are going to show your business plan to people outside of your business, including family or friends, you need to take some steps to ensure that the way it's put together reflects the work that has been carried out and the value of your proposition. If you take it seriously you can expect others to do the same.

Packaging

Appropriate packaging enhances every product, and a business plan is no exception. A simple spiral binding with a plastic cover on the front and back makes it easy for the reader to move from section to section, and it ensures the plan will survive frequent handling.

Writing clearly

You and any partners should write the first draft of the business plan yourselves. The niceties of grammar and style can be resolved later. When your first draft has been revised, then comes the task of editing. Here the grammar, spelling and language must be carefully checked to ensure that your business plan is crisp, correct, clear and complete – and not too long: *circa* 10–15 pages will be more than sufficient in most cases.

A 'prospectus', such as a business plan seeking finance from investors, can have a legal status, turning any claims you may make for sales and profits (for example) into a 'contract'. Your accountant and legal adviser will be able to help you with the appropriate language that can convey your projections without giving them contractual status.

This would also be a good time to talk over the proposal with a 'friendly' financier. He or she can give an insider's view as to the strengths and weaknesses of your proposal.

Presentation techniques

If getting someone interested in your business plan is half the battle in raising funds, the other half is the oral presentation. Any organization financing a venture will insist on seeing the person or team involved presenting and defending the plans. They know that they are backing people every bit as much as the idea. You can be sure that any financier you are presenting to will be well prepared.

Keep these points in mind when preparing for the presentation of your business plan:

- Find out how much time you have; then rehearse your presentation beforehand. Allow at least as much time for questions as for your talk.
- Use visual aids and if possible bring and demonstrate your product or service. A video or computer-generated model is better than nothing.
- Explain your strategy in a businesslike manner, demonstrating your grasp of the competitive market forces at work. Listen to comments and criticisms carefully, avoiding a defensive attitude when you respond.
- Make your replies to questions brief and to the point. If they want more information, they can ask. This approach allows time for the many different questions that must be asked, either now or later, before an investment can proceed.
- Your goal is to create empathy between yourself and your listener(s). While you may not be able to change your personality, you could take a few tips on presentation skills. Eye contact, tone of speech, enthusiasm and body language all have a part to play in making a presentation successful.
- Wearing a suit is never likely to upset anyone. Shorts and sandals could just set the wrong tone! Serious money calls for serious people.
- Be prepared. You need to have every aspect of your business plan in your head and know your way around the plan forwards, backwards and sideways! You never know when the chance to present may occur. It's as well to have a 5-, 10- and 20-minute presentation ready to run at a moment's notice.

Making an elevator pitch

Often the person you are pitching your proposal to is short of time. As a rough rule of thumb, the closer you get to an individual with the power to make decisions the less time you will get to make your pitch. So you need to have a short presentation to hand that can be made in any circumstance – in a plane, at an airport or between floors in a lift: hence the name 'elevator pitch'.

Using a non-disclosure agreement (NDA)

If you are going to show or discuss your business plan with business partners and it contains confidential information on your business or on the development of a unique idea, you should consider getting them to sign an NDA. NDAs are confidentiality agreements that bind recipients to maintain your 'secrets' and not to take any action that could damage the value of the 'secrets'.

This means that they can't share the information with anyone else or act on the idea themselves, for a period of time at least. NDAs are a helpful way of getting advice and help whilst protecting you from someone using your information to compete against you. Business Link (www.businesslink.gov.uk > Exploit your ideas > Protecting your intellectual property > Non-disclosure agreements) provides more information on this subject, as well as a web link to a free sample NDA.

4

Dealing with regulatory authorities

12

Computing taxes

The more successful a business is, the greater its exposure to tax liabilities. Its exact tax position will depend on the legal nature of the business. A limited company is subject to corporation tax at a set rate announced each year by the Government. If the business is not a limited company, its proprietor is likely to be subject to income tax and to tax rates applying to the general public. Simply monitoring pre-tax ratios provides satisfactory measures of trading performance, but this is not enough. The owner/manager will be concerned with the net profit *after tax*, as this is the money that is available to help the business to grow or to overcome unforeseen problems.

Managing the tax position is one area where professional advice is essential. This is very important, as tax rules can change every year. Good advice can help to reduce the overall tax bill and so increase the value of profits to the business.

A business has three broad responsibilities when it comes to taxation:

1. to pay tax on business profits;
2. to pay Value Added Tax (VAT) based on turnover;
3. to collect and pay tax and National Insurance on behalf of everyone employed in the business.

Sole traders and partnerships are treated differently to limited companies for tax purposes, so we will look at each in turn.

Sole traders and partnerships

Partnerships are treated as a collection of sole traders for tax purposes, and each partner's share of that collective liability has to be worked out. Sole (self-employed) traders have all their income from every source brought together and taxed as one entity. In the United Kingdom, the taxes that need to be calculated are:

- income tax, paid on profits;
- Class 4 National Insurance, paid on profits;
- Capital Gains Tax, paid on the disposal of fixed assets at a profit, or when the business is sold;
- inheritance tax, paid on death or when certain gifts are made.

Neither of the last two taxes are likely to occur on a regular basis, so we will not be dealing with them. When those taxes do come into play, the sums involved are likely to be significant and professional advice should be taken from the outset.

Income tax

The profit-and-loss account structure that we looked at earlier, while more than adequate for the purpose of running a business, is not quite sufficient for working out the likely amount of tax due. Some perfectly proper expenses that we need to account for in deciding how well (or badly) a business is performing are not allowed for tax purposes. For example, entertainment costs would appear in the management accounts, but the cost would not be allowed for tax purposes.

The rate of depreciation, for example, is a matter for each businessperson to decide for him- or herself. In the management accounts you can decide, for example, to depreciate an asset over one year or five years. The nominal effect on profits can be significant.

Certain business expenses are disallowed, partially disallowed or allowed for, but in a different way. The same methods are used by tax authorities throughout the world. After you have produced your management accounts showing what you understand to be the income and expenditure for the period to be, and have compiled a record of assets bought, a process known as a 'profit computation' has to be carried out. This adjusts that profit figure to meet the tax authorities' needs. Unsurprisingly, this will almost inevitably be a higher figure, and so have a higher tax liability, than the one that you will have arrived at in your management accounts.

In the computation, some expenses are disallowed. These include depreciation, which has been replaced by capital allowances. Capital allowances are an incentive offered by governments to encourage investment in new equipment and technology. The rate is changed in the annual budget to reflect the foibles of the government of the day.

The writing down allowance, as the capital allowance is commonly known, varies according to the item concerned, the size of business, the economic climate and other Treasury-determined limiting factors. For example, motor cars can be written down at 25 per cent of the declining balance of the original cost up to a maximum of £3,000 a year. So if you buy a car costing £20,000, although theoretically £5,000 can be charged against tax, in practice only £3,000 will be allowed. A small company can write plant and machinery down by 50 per cent in the year of purchase, a medium-sized firm by 40 per cent and a large firm by 25 per cent. These complexities certainly keep tax accountants in regular work!

The changes that have to be made to the management accounts to arrive at the profit for tax purposes can have a significant effect on the end result. You will need to ensure that any expense that may have seemed reasonable in the management accounts meets the more stringent requirements of the tax authorities. You are generally allowed to set an expense against your income if it is:

- incurred wholly and exclusively for the purposes of trade;
- properly charged against income (not, for example, purchase of a property lease, which is capital);
- not specifically disallowed by statute (for example, you cannot set entertainment of customers against your tax, although it is a perfectly legitimate accounting expense).

Net taxable profit

Under the self-assessment tax system in the United Kingdom, the basis of the period of a year of assessment is the accounting year ending within that tax year. So if you made up your accounts to 31 December, the basis period for income tax year 2007/2008 would be 6 April 2007 to 5 April 2008. There are special rules that apply for the first year and the last year of trading that should ensure that tax is charged fairly.

If your turnover is low – currently in the United Kingdom, less than £15,000 per year – you can put in a three-line account: sales, expenses and profit. If it is over the current low figure, you have to summarize your accounts to show turnover, gross profit and expenses by main heading.

You will have a personal allowance (the current threshold below which you don't pay tax). That amount is deducted from the profit figure. Then a figure is added for Class 4 National Insurance based on taxable profits that lie within a certain band. In the United Kingdom, that band is currently between about £5,225 and £34,840 and the tax rate is 8 per cent. This is paid in addition to the flat rate Class 2 contributions of about £2.20 per week.

All these rates and amounts are constantly changing, but the broad principles remain. Check out the HM Revenue & Customs (HMRC) website (www.hmrc.gov.uk) for the current position with regard to all tax and VAT thresholds and rates.

Company taxation

Companies have a separate legal identity from those who work for them, whether or not they are shareholding directors. Everyone working for the business is taxed as an employee. UK companies are responsible for collecting tax and passing it to the tax authorities through the PAYE (pay as you earn) system.

Directors' pay is a business expense, just as with any other wage, and is deducted from the company's revenue when calculating its taxable profits.

Companies in the United Kingdom pay tax in three main ways:

1. On the company's profits for the year, as calculated in the tax-adjusted profits. This is called 'corporation tax'. The rate of corporation tax in the United Kingdom, and in many other countries, depends on the amount of profit made. If the profit is less than £300,000, the small companies rate of 20 per cent applies. If the profit is above £1.5 million, the full rate of 30 per cent is charged. For figures in between, a taper applies. All these figures are subject to annual review in the budget. Corporation tax is payable nine months after the end of the accounting period.
2. On the distribution of profit to the shareholders in the dividend payment. This gives the appearance of taxing the same profit twice, but through a process of 'tax credits', this double taxation doesn't generally occur. When a shareholder gets a dividend from a company, it comes with a tax

credit attached. This means that any shareholder on the basic rate of tax won't have to pay any further tax. Higher-rate tax payers, however, have a further amount of tax to pay.

3. On capital gains. If an asset – say, a business property – is sold at a profit, then the company will have made a capital gain. This gain will be taxed along the general lines of corporation tax, but with lower rates applying to smaller companies.

As tax is a business expense for a company, an allowance for tax must be included in the accounts. When it's paid it will appear in the profit-and-loss account. Before it is paid we 'accrue' for it by showing it as a creditor in the balance sheet (an accrual is the process of managing a business event that is not documented). Generally, people send companies bills for all services rendered, so that is the 'document' in the company accounts. But where no document exists – as with tax due – yet it is recognized that the business owes the money, it is accrued for.

Which structure is best?

A company's financial affairs are in the public domain. As well as keeping HMRC informed, companies have to file their accounts with Companies House (www.companieshouse.gov.uk/about/gbhtml/gb3.shtml). Accounts should be filed within 10 months of the company's financial year end. Small businesses (turnover below £5.6 million) can file abbreviated accounts that include only very limited balance sheet and profit-and-loss account information, and these do not need to be audited. You can be fined up to £1,000 for filing accounts late.

The most important rule is: never let the 'tax tail wag the business dog'. Tax is just one aspect of business life. If you want to keep your business's finances private, then the public filing of accounts required of companies is not for you. On the other hand, if you feel that you want to protect your private assets from creditors if things go wrong, then being a sole trader or partner is probably not the best route to take.

Company profits and losses are locked into the company, so if you have several lines of business using different trading entities you cannot easily offset losses in one area against profits in another. But as sole traders are treated as one entity for all their sources of income, there is more scope for netting off gains and losses. Some points to bear in mind here are:

- If your profits are likely to be small, say below £50,000, for some time, then from a purely tax point of view you may pay less as a sole trader. This is because, as an individual, you get a tax-free allowance – your first few thousand pounds of income are not taxable. This amount varies according to personal circumstances – whether you are married or single, for example – and can be changed in the budget each year.
- If you expect to be making higher rates of profit, say above £50,000, and want to reinvest a large portion of those profits back into your business, then you could be better off forming a company, as companies don't start paying higher rates of tax until their profits are £300,000. Even then, companies don't pay the 40 per cent tax rate that a sole trader would if he or she were to make a profit above £30,000, taking allowances into account. So, a company making £300,000 taxable profits could have £54,000 more profit to reinvest in financing future outgoings than a sole trader in the same line of work (£240,000–£186,000).
- Non-salary benefits favour the sole trader. It is generally possible to get tax relief on the business element of costs that are only partly business related, such a running a vehicle. The director of a company would be taxed on the value of the vehicle's list price and would not be allowed travel to and from work as a business expense.

Minimizing taxes

There is no need to pay more tax than you have to. While staying within the law by a safe margin, you should explore ways to avoid as oppose to *evade* tax liability. This is a complex area and one subject to frequent change. The tax authorities constantly try to close loopholes in the tax system, whilst highly paid tax accountants and lawyers try even harder to find new ways around the rules. These are some of the areas to keep in mind when assessing your tax liability:

- Make sure you have included all allowable business expenses, especially if you have recently set up a business, as you may not be fully aware of all the expenses that can be claimed. For example, while entertaining clients is not an allowable business expense, the cost of your meals may well be allowable if you are away from home and staying overnight. Bytestart.co.uk, the small business portal, has a useful busienss expenses guide (www.bytestart.co.uk > Money & tax > Business expenses guide).

- If you have made losses in any tax period, these may, under certain circumstances, be carried forward to offset future taxable profits or backwards against past profits.
- Capital Gains Tax can be deferred if another asset is to be bought with the proceeds. This is known as *rollover relief* and it can normally be used up to three years after the taxable event.
- Top up or start a pension, as you can put up to £215,000 or your profits, whichever is the lower, in and so avoid paying up to £86,000 of tax. If you take out a Self Invest Personal Pension Scheme (SIPPS) you can invest the proceeds in most types of business premises, a shop, warehouse, office or workshop. Before you take the plunge, get professional advice from a tax expert and a pension provider. To find out more about SIPPS, you could contact the Pensions Advisory Service (TPAS), an independent non-profit organisation and a good place to head for general information (tel: 0845 601 2923; www.opas.org.uk); the Association of Independent Financial Advisors (tel: 020 7628 1287; www.aifa.net); and the directory of UK tax professionals at TaxationWeb (www.taxationweb.co.uk/directory).
- If you do intend to buy capital assets for your business, bring forward your spending plans to maximize the use of the writing-down allowance.
- Identify non-cash benefits that you and others working for you could take instead of taxable salary. For employees, a share-option scheme may achieve the same, or better, level of reward with less tax payable.
- Examine the pros and cons of taking your money out of a limited company by dividends or salary. These are taxed differently and may provide scope for tax reduction.
- If your spouse has no other income from employment, they could earn a sum equivalent to their annual tax-free allowance (currently about £4,000) by working for your business.
- Have you any pre-trading expenses incurred at any stage over the seven years before you started up the business? They can probably be treated as if they had been incurred after trading started. Such items may include the cost of carrying out market research, designing and testing your product or service, and capital items such as a computer bought before you started trading, which was then brought into the assets of your business.
- Have you bought any business assets on hire purchase? You may be able to treat the full purchase price in your capital allowances calculation.

This is an indicative rather than a comprehensive list of areas to explore. Tax is a field in which timely professional advice can produce substantial benefits in the form of lower tax bills.

Dealing with employment taxes

As an employer – and as a director of a limited company you may well be your own employee – you are responsible for collecting and paying the following taxes.

PAYE (Pay As You Earn)

Employers are responsible for deducting income tax from employees' accounts and making the relevant payment to HMRC. If you trade as a limited company, then as a director any salary you receive will be subject to PAYE. You will need to work out the tax due. HMRC (www.hmrc.gov.uk/employers/employers-pack.htm) gives details on PAYE in their employer pack.

National Insurance (NI)

Almost everyone who works has to pay a separate tax, National Insurance, collected by HMRC, which, in theory at least, goes towards the state pension and other benefits. NI is paid at different rates, and self-employed people pay Class 4 contributions calculated each year on the self-assessment tax form.

The amount of National Insurance paid depends on a mass of different factors, such as those that apply to married women, volunteer development workers, share fishermen, the self-employed and those with small earnings, which attract NI rates of between 1 and 12 per cent. HMRC (www.hmrc.gov.uk > Library > Rates & allowances > National Insurance contributions) provides tables showing the current contribution rates, and elsewhere on the site (www.hmrc.gov.uk > Employers > National Insurance) you can download an employer's annual pack with all the complexities of NI paperwork.

Value added tax (VAT)

VAT is a tax on consumer spending. It is a European tax system, although most countries have significant variations in VAT rates, starting thresholds and in the schemes themselves. It effectively requires every business over a certain size to become a tax collector. There is no reward for carrying out this task, but there are penalties for making mistakes or for making late VAT returns.

VAT is complicated tax. Essentially, you must register if your taxable turnover (ie sales, not profit) exceeds £67,000 in any 12-month period, or if it looks as though it might reasonably be expected to do so. This rate is reviewed each year in the budget and is frequently changed. The United Kingdom is significantly out of line with many other countries in Europe, where VAT entry rates are much lower. The general rule is that all supplies of goods and services are taxable at the standard rate – 17.5 per cent – unless they are specifically stated by the law to be zero-rated or exempt. When deciding whether your turnover exceeds the limit you have to include zero-rated sales (things like most foods, books and children's clothing) as they are *technically* taxable – however, their rate of tax is 0 per cent. You leave out exempt items. There are three free booklets issued by HMRC: a simple introductory booklet called *Should You be Registered for VAT?* and two more detailed booklets called *General Guide* and *Scope and Coverage*. If in doubt (the language is not easy to understand), ask your accountant or the local branch of HMRC – after all, they would rather help you to get it right in the first place than have to sort it out later when you make a mess of it.

Each quarter, you will have to complete a return, which shows your purchases and the VAT you paid on them, and your sales and the VAT you collected on them. The VAT taxes paid and collected are offset against one another and the balance is sent to HMRC. If you have paid more VAT in any one quarter than you have collected, you will get a refund. For this reason, it sometimes pays to register even if you don't have to – if you are selling mostly zero-rated items for example. Also, being registered for VAT may make your business appear more professional to your potential customers.

VAT records

The bookkeeping system that we started out with may need to be extended to accommodate VAT records. So the analysed cash book, if we are using a simple system, may look like Table 12.1.

You can see that the single figure for the amount paid used in the pre-VAT registration bookkeeping system has been replaced by three columns. One shows the amount before VAT is charged, then the amount of the VAT, followed by the gross amount including VAT. The analysis columns contain the net amounts. You can cross-check the arithmetic by totalling the three columns of

Table 12.1 Value Added Tax bookkeeping records, payments

Payments			*Reference number*	*Net amount (£)*	*VAT at 17.5% (£)*	*Gross amount (£)*	*Analysis*		
Date	*Name*	*Details*					*Stocks*	*Vehicles*	*Telephone*
4 June	Gibbs	Stock purchase	001	263.83	46.17	310.00	263.83		
8 June	Gibbs	Stock purchase	002	110.64	19.36	130.00	110.64		
12 June	ABC Telecoms	Telephone charges	003	47.00	8.23	55.23			47.00
18 June	Colt Rentals	Vehicle hire	004	74.26	13.00	87.26		74.26	
22 June	VV Mobiles	Mobile phone	005	45.31	7.93	53.24			45.31
27 June	Gibbs	Stock purchase	006	30.88	5.40	36.28	30.88		
Totals				**571.92**	**100.09**	**672.01**	**405.35**	**74.26**	**92.31**

analysis and confirming that they add up to the total of the net amount; in this example, £571.92.

The same layout can be used for bookkeeping records of receipts, with or without the analysis.

Doing the sum

Calculating the VAT of any transaction can be a confusing sum. These simple rules will help you to get it right every time. Take the gross amount of any sum (the total, including any VAT) and divide it into 117.5 parts if the VAT rate is 17.5 per cent (if the VAT rate is not 17.5 per cent, use the figure that corresponds to the VAT rate plus 100). All this means is that we are saying that the bill we have received is 100 per cent of the net bill with another 17.5 per cent added on top.

Then we can take a 117.5th part of the bill and multiply it by 100 to get the pre-VAT total and multiply by 17.5 to arrive at the VAT element of the bill (see Figure 12.1).

Net amount (£)	VAT at 17.5% (£)		Gross amount (£)	
			310	
			divided by 117.5 =	
263.83	46.17	◄ = 17.5 ×	2.64	×100 =

Figure 12.1 Calculating VAT sums

Doing the VAT return

This has to be where a computer-based bookkeeping system wins hands down. VAT returns (or 'sales tax returns' in the United States) can be automatically generated by an accounting package. When using such a package, all you have to do is enter the current VAT rate. If you take Web-enabled software updates, you may not even have to do this. Basically, the VAT inspectors are interested in five figures (see Figure 12.2):

- how much VAT you have collected on their behalf on the goods and services you have sold;
- how much VAT has been collected from you by those who have sold you goods and services;

The difference between those two sums is, if positive, the VAT due to be paid, or, if negative, the amount of VAT to be reclaimed. For businesses VAT is a zero sum game, it's the end consumer who picks up the tab.

The final two numbers are a check on the reasonableness of the whole sum. Here you must show the value of your sales and purchases net of VAT for the period in question. The VAT return has to be signed by the person registered for VAT. It's important to remember that a named person is responsible for VAT, as a limited company is treated as a 'person' in this instance. Not only does it act as an unpaid tax collector but there are penalties for filing a return late or incorrectly. VAT records have to be kept for six years and periodically you can expect a visit from a VAT inspector.

Payment methods

Normally VAT is paid each quarter, but small businesses can take advantage of a number of schemes to simplify procedures or aid their cash flow. The annual accounting scheme open to businesses with annual turnover up to £1,350,000

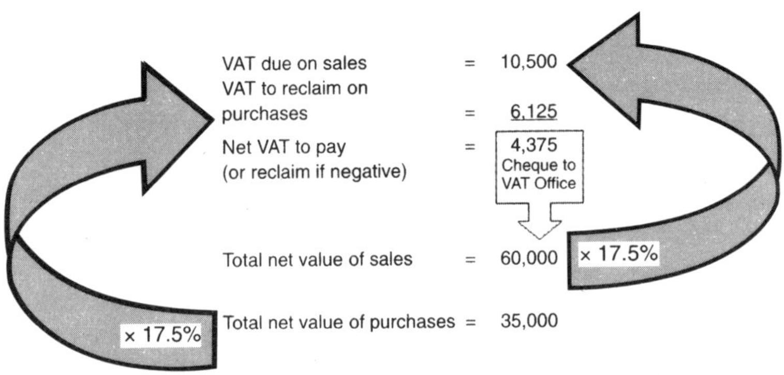

Figure 12.2 The essence of the VAT return

lets you pay monthly or quarterly estimated figures, submitting a single annual return at the end of the year with any balancing payment. The cash accounting scheme available to similarly sized businesses allows you to delay paying over any VAT until you have actually collected it from your customers. The flat-rate scheme allows businesses with annual turnover up to £150,000 to calculate their VAT as a flat percentage of total sales, rather than having to record the VAT charged on individual purchases and sales.

Other matters

We have only sketched an outline of VAT here. There are a number of special schemes for retailers, adjustments to be made for any private usage, different ways of handling certain second-hand goods and scale charges to be applied to the use of motor vehicles. So, it is advisable to get the free booklets on offer from the VAT authorities and to take professional advice if you have any doubts.

You will be given a VAT number when you register, which should be stated on all your invoices. If you suspect a business charging you VAT is not registered or that one should be, you can contact HMRC's National Advice Service on 0845 010 900. You can verify European VAT numbers at the European Commission website (http://ec.europa.eu > Taxation and Customs Union > VIES).

The way VAT is handled on goods and services sold to and bought from other European countries is subject to another set of rules and procedures. HMRC (www.hmrc.gov.uk > Businesses and corporations > VAT) publishes a series of guides such as *Should you be registered for VAT?* and a general guide.

Surviving a tax investigation

If your books are in good order and you honestly report your income and expenses you should have little trouble from the authorities. However, there are serious penalties for tax misdemeanours, and you are required to keep your accounts for six years, so at any point should tax authorities become suspicious they can dig into the past even after they have agreed your figures. In the case of suspected fraud there is no limit to how far back the digging can go.

There are a variety of reasons a tax investigation can be triggered, ranging from the banal to the frankly terrifying. A number of businesses are put under the spotlight each year, and you could just be pulled out of the hat. Or you could be in an industry that for one reason or another is being generally investigated. It is more likely, however, either that your accounts have shown some major and unexplained changes (unusually high expenses, for example) or that you have been noticed for having a lifestyle inconsistent with the profits you are reporting. This could come about through a diligent tax inspector, an envious neighbour, a disgruntled former spouse or employee, or indiscreet gossip in the pub.

However it is triggered, you need professional advice from your accountant immediately. It would certainly be prudent to protect yourself from some problems by getting insurance against a tax, VAT or NI investigation. The Association of British Insurers (www.abi.org.uk) can put you in contact with a source of such insurance.

Help and advice with tax matters

Business Link has a beginner's guide to tax and accounts in the form of a series of questions at the end of which you get a report telling you about the tax you have to pay and the accounts you have to keep (www.businesslink.gov.uk > Taxes, returns & payroll > Introduction to business taxes > Beginner's guide to tax and accounts).

HMRC has online guides for employers, businesses and corporations linked directly from its home page (www.hmrc.gov.uk). Taxcafe (www.taxcafe.co.uk > UK taxes > Corporation and business taxes) has a series of guides priced at around £25 each on such subjects as using a company to save tax, and salary versus dividends, and a tax and VAT question-and-answer service, where for £90 you can ask any question and get an answer within three to five working days.

Finding a low-tax country

Most countries have some form of taxation, and the rules are often different for foreigners who invest in the country. There is usually no way of avoiding paying taxes somewhere, but you do have some choice as to where you end up paying and hence the amount of tax you pay. The governing rule on who you pay your taxes to is not so much about where you live, or necessarily where your income comes from, as where you are resident. The word 'resident' has a particular meaning when it comes to taxation and is not necessarily the same as having a residence card or living in the country.

Taking up residence

If you have been living and paying taxes say in the United Kingdom, then simply going overseas will not change the fact that you are 'ordinarily resident' in the United Kingdom. If you leave the United Kingdom to take up permanent residence abroad and so inform HMRC, they will normally accept this at face value and treat you as ceasing to be resident on the day following your departure. If you spend an average of 91 days or more per year in the United Kingdom, over any four-year period, you will be swept back into the United Kingdom tax net. You are, since a rule change in 1993, even allowed to have accommodation available for your use in the United Kingdom.

Double taxation agreements

It is possible to be tax resident in both countries if you meet both sets of rules. For example, if you spend 200 days abroad in your chosen country of residence, 100 days in the United Kingdom and the remaining days elsewhere, both the foreign and the UK tax authorities or your home tax authority could reasonably lay claim to you. Most countries have 'double taxation' agreements that are designed to settle the argument. 'Tie breakers', as the relevant clauses in the double taxation agreement are known, deal with such cases as those where people have homes, assets and income in roughly equal proportions in both countries. In those circumstances you are deemed normally to be a resident of the country of which you are a national.

The aim of double taxation agreements is to help make sure that you don't pay tax on the same taxable event twice, once in a foreign country and again at home. But you could well end up paying different taxes in each country.

The key taxes to consider

- *General income tax.* This is a tax on income earned in a particular country from employment or any profitable activity. Some countries operate a flat-rate structure, such as Estonia where 23 per cent is applied on all income. Other countries, such as New Zealand and Morocco, have a sliding rate with a 0 per cent band, while Thailand and Mexico tax even the lowest earners. The Netherlands, Denmark, Spain, Austria, Slovenia and China tax even fairly modest levels of income at between 45 and 59 per cent.

- *Income from investments.* In many countries, but not all, this falls into the same bands as for personal taxation.
- *Business tax.* This varies widely around the world. The Maldives (9 per cent) and the United Arab Emirates (15 per cent) are towards the low end of the scale, while Italy (76 per cent) and India (81 per cent) are among countries with the highest business taxes. All business taxes are complicated, but in some countries they are more complicated than in others. For example, it takes over 1,000 hours to prepare and file all business taxes in countries such as Ukraine, Brazil and the Czech Republic, while in Singapore, Switzerland and the Seychelles the whole task can be completed in less than 70 hours.
- *Capital gains tax.* This is the tax charged against the profit or gain made on the disposal of an investment in an asset, such as a business. As with other taxes, there are a wide variety of rates and conditions to look out for. You can usually reclaim any capital gains tax paid if a reinvestment is made within a set period.
- *Value added and sales taxes.* These are taxes levied on transactions rather than on income earned. Within Europe these taxes are levied at widely different rates, anything between 15 per cent and 22 per cent being the norm. Canada's VAT rate of 7 per cent is one of the lowest, and Brazil's and Denmark's 25 per cent the highest. In addition some items are exempt from this tax in some countries.
- *Import duties.* Within the European Union import duties are largely a thing of the past. Also, many countries exempt personal effects brought into a country, including furniture, computers and even motor vehicles. But not all countries are equally forgiving. For example, you can import virtually anything into Iraq free of import duties, while anything taken into the Dominican Republic will be liable to a local tax of up to 40 per cent.
- *Tax holidays and inducements to invest.* Many countries offer individuals and businesses tax or grant inducements to buy business assets in certain areas. These are often short-lived opportunities, and like all such offers are intended to encourage some risk taking. The degree of risk and reward varies enormously.
- *Annual property tax.* Simply owning a property usually lands either the owner or the occupants with a tax bill, which can be either nominal (Bulgaria) or prohibitive (the United Kingdom).

- *Wealth tax ('capital tax', 'equity tax', 'net worth tax' and 'net wealth tax').* Countries such as Finland, France, Greece, Iceland, Luxembourg, Norway, Spain, Sweden and Switzerland levy a tax each year on the value of their citizens' assets. In some cases, in France for example, the reach of the tax goes further still; anyone resident in France on 1 January is taxable on his or her worldwide assets, and non-residents with assets in France are taxed on the value of their French assets as at 1 January each year. France assesses annually, with progressive rates ranging from 0.55 to 1.8 per cent for people whose worldwide assets are greater than €732,000. In Iceland you only need to have net assets in excess of €53,000 to become caught up in the wealth tax net.
- *Inheritance tax and death duties.* You will have to consider who inherits when you or any joint owner of the business dies and set this out in a will. If you don't, the death in question will be dealt with under the intestacy laws, which are a nightmare to deal with, especially if there is scope for ambiguity as to whether the matter should be dealt with under British law or the law of the country in question. Unlike the position under UK law, under the law of many overseas countries certain family members have automatic inheritance rights. For example, spouses and children, even illegitimate ones, may not be cut out of a will. However, if you are still a British citizen, irrespective of your tax residency arrangements, your will, as long as you make one, will usually be dealt with under UK law. While a UK will is usually valid under the law in most foreign countries, it is advisable to draw up a will in the country in question to save time in being able to distribute the estate and the ensuing additional administrative costs. Your foreign and UK wills must not conflict in any way; otherwise that will leave scope for interminable disputes, time delays and additional costs. You will need an executor for your foreign will. While in the United Kingdom it is not uncommon for lay people to act as executors, proving a will abroad, especially for a foreigner, can be complex, so it may make good sense to appoint a local lawyer to steer the inheritors in the best direction.

Sources of help, advice and information on foreign tax

- The American Council for Capital Formation (www.accf.org/publications/reports/sr-intcomp-deathtax.html). This link is to a table showing an international comparison of inheritance taxes. Japan has the highest rate (70 per cent), followed by the United States (55 per cent), with the

United Kingdom and France coming in at 40 per cent. The starting point for levying the tax ranges from the relatively low figure of €30,000 in Denmark up to $3 million in the United States.

- Doing Business (www.doingbusiness.org). From the left-hand vertical menu bar select 'Paying taxes'. From there you will find the taxes that a small to medium-size business must pay or withhold in a given year, as well as measures of administrative burden in paying taxes. The opening table in this section shows the total number of taxes paid, the time it takes to prepare, file and pay (or withhold) the relevant tax, the value added tax and social security contributions (in hours per year), and total amount of taxes payable by the business, except for labour taxes. To see the full details of the tax regime for a specific country, use the drop-down box on the top right of the screen or click on the relevant country link on that page. By clicking on the column headers you can sort the relevant data to show, for example, which country has the highest or lowest taxes, requires the most or least time to deal with taxes, or involves the most or fewest separate tax payments.
- HMRC (www.hmrc.gov.uk > Practitioner zone > A–Z list > Double taxation treaty; www.hmrc.gov.uk > Practitioner zone > A–Z list > Residency > Residency and domicile issues) provides the UK perspective on these issues.
- The International Tax Planning Association (www.itpa.org > The ITPA Green Book) is a directory of tax advisory organizations searchable by jurisdiction.
- The Wealth Protection Report (www.wealthprotectionreport.co.uk > Non UK domicile status) is a series of articles on offshore tax planning.
- Worldwide Tax (www.worldwide-tax.com). From the central menu on the home page select 'Tax rates around the world – comparison' to find a quick summary of income and corporate tax levels, as well as value added tax, for all the countries covered. From the vertical menu bar on the left of the home page screen select from the 'Shortcut to countries' section the countries you are interested in researching. Once in the country page, scroll down to the country taxes menu in the centre of the page and select the appropriate tax. At the bottom of that menu you can select 'Tax news' for the current year, where you will find the latest changes in tax rules for the country in question.

13

Alternative legal structures

Their impact on financial procedures

You will need to consider which of the four main legal forms your business will take. The one you choose will depend on a number of factors: commercial needs, financial risk, the requirement for outside capital and your tax position. You will almost certainly need to change legal forms one or more times as the business grows and takes on employees and managers.

Each of these forms is explained briefly below, together with the procedure to follow on setting them up. You can change your ownership status later as your circumstances change, so while this is an important decision, it is not a final one.

Sole traders

Over 80 per cent of businesses start up as sole traders and indeed around 55 per cent of all businesses employing fewer than 50 people still use this legal structure. It has the merit of being relatively formality free and, unless you intend to register for VAT, there are few rules about the records you have to keep. There is no requirement for your accounts to be audited or for financial information on your business to be filed at Companies House.

For a sole trader there is no legal distinction between you and your business – your business is one of your assets, just as your house or car is. It follows from this that if your business should fail, your creditors have a right not only to the assets of the business but also to your personal assets, subject only to the provisions of the Bankruptcy Acts (these allow you to keep only a few absolutely basic essentials for yourself and your family).

It is possible to avoid the worst of these consequences by ensuring that your private assets are the legal property of your spouse, against whom your creditors have no claim. (You must be solvent when the transfer is made, and that transfer must have been made at least two years prior to your business running into trouble.) However, to be effective such a transfer must be absolute and you can have no say in how your spouse chooses to dispose of his or her new-found wealth!

The capital to get the business going must come from you – or from loans. There is no access to equity capital, which has the attraction of being risk-free. In return for these drawbacks you can have the pleasure of being your own boss immediately, subject only to declaring your profits on your tax return.

Partnerships and limited partnerships

Partnerships are effectively collections of sole traders and, as such, share the legal problems attached to personal liability. There are very few restrictions to setting up in business with another person (or persons) in partnership, and several definite advantages. By pooling resources you may have access to more capital; you will be bringing, hopefully, several sets of skills to the business; and if you are ill the business can still carry on.

There are two serious drawbacks that you should certainly consider. First, if your partner makes a business mistake, perhaps by signing a disastrous contract, without your knowledge or consent, every member of the partnership must shoulder the consequences. Under these circumstances your personal assets could be taken to pay the creditors even though the mistake was no fault of your own.

Second, if your partner goes bankrupt in his or her personal capacity, for whatever reason, his or her share of the partnership can be seized by creditors. As a private individual you are not liable for your partner's private debts, but having to buy him or her out of the partnership at short notice could put you and the business in financial jeopardy. Even death may not release you from partnership obligations, and in some circumstances your estate can remain liable. Unless you take 'public' leave of your partnership by notifying your business contacts and legally bringing your partnership to an end, you could remain liable.

The legal regulations governing this field are set out in the Partnership Act 1890, which in essence assumes that competent businesspeople should know what they are doing. The Act merely provides a framework of agreement that applies 'in the absence of agreement to the contrary'. It follows from this that many partnerships are entered into without legal formalities – and sometimes without the parties themselves being aware that they have entered a partnership!

The main provisions of the Partnership Act state:

- All partners contribute capital equally.
- All partners share profits and losses equally.
- No partner shall have interest paid on his capital.
- No partner shall be paid a salary.
- All partners have an equal say in the management of the business.

It is unlikely that all these provisions will suit you, so you would be well advised to get a 'partnership agreement' drawn up in writing by a solicitor at the outset of your venture.

One possibility that can reduce the more painful consequences of entering a partnership as a 'sleeping partner' is to have your involvement registered as a limited partnership. It means you (or your partner) can play no active part in running the business, but your risks are limited to the capital that you put in.

Unless you are a member of certain professions (eg law, accountancy, etc) you are restricted to a maximum of 20 partners in any partnership.

Limited companies

In the United Kingdom, before the 1895 Companies Act it was necessary to have an Act of Parliament or a Royal Charter in order to set up a company. Now, out of the 4.5 million businesses trading in the United Kingdom, over 1.4 million are limited companies. As the name suggests, in this form of business your liability is limited to the amount you state that you will contribute by way of share capital. (Though you may not actually have to put that money in!)

A limited company has a legal identity of its own, separate from the people who own or run it. This means that, in the event of failure, creditors' claims are restricted to the assets of the company. The shareholders of the business are not liable as individuals for the business debts beyond the paid-up value of their shares. This applies even if the shareholders are working directors, unless of course the company has been trading fraudulently. (In practice, the ability to limit liability is severely restricted these days, as most lenders, including the banks, often insist on personal guarantees from the directors.) The main advantage from a financial perspective is the freedom to raise capital by selling shares to others willing to join in the risk of the venture. For the business this is a safer way of funding than borrowing money, which in any event has to be returned and will during the life of the loan attract a changing burden of interest. Shareholders can of course also seek to get their investment out, but they usually have to look to another third party to take over their stake: the company is under no obligation to pay shareholders back until the business is wound up.

Disadvantages include the cost involved in setting up the company and the legal requirement in some cases for the company's accounts to be audited by a chartered or certified accountant. Usually it is only businesses with assets approaching £3 million that have to be audited, but if, for example, you have shareholders who own more than 10 per cent of your firm, they can ask for the accounts to be audited. You can find out the latest information on auditing small firms either from your accountant or on the Business Link website (www.businesslink.gov.uk > Taxes, returns and payroll > Introduction to business taxes > Accounting and audit exemptions for small companies).

A limited company can be formed by two shareholders, one of whom must be a director. A company secretary must also be appointed, who can be a shareholder, director, or outside person such as an accountant or lawyer.

The company can be bought 'off the shelf' from a registration agent and then adapted to suit your own purposes. This will involve changing the name, shareholders and articles of association, and will cost about £250 and take a couple of weeks to arrange. Alternatively, you can form your own company, using your solicitor or accountant. This will cost around £500 and take six to eight weeks.

The behaviour of companies and their directors is governed by the various Companies Acts that have come into effect since 1844, the latest of which came into effect in November 2006.

Cooperatives

A cooperative is an enterprise owned and controlled by the people working in it. Once in danger of becoming extinct, the workers' cooperative is enjoying something of a comeback, and there are over 4,370 operating in the United Kingdom, employing 195,000 people. They are growing at the rate of 20 per cent per annum.

Help and advice on business ownership matters

- A guidance note entitled 'Business ownership' is available from Companies House (www.companieshouse.gov.uk > Guidance booklets).
- Business Link (www.businesslink.gov.uk > Taxes, returns and payroll > Choosing and setting up a legal structure > Legal structure: the basics) has a guide to putting your business on a proper legal footing, explaining the tax and other implications of different ownership structures.
- Co-operatives UK (www.cooperatives-uk.coop > Services > Co-operative development) is the central membership organization for cooperative enterprises throughout the United Kingdom. This link is to the regional network.
- Desktop Lawyer (www.desktoplawyer.co.uk > Business > Business start-up > Choosing a business structure > The partnership) has a summary of the pros and cons of partnerships, as well as inexpensive partnership deeds.

14

Directors' roles and responsibilities

While most businesses start out as sole traders or partnerships, those that grow to any size or complexity, require substantial investment or need to share the ownership rewards with a team of managers will end up as limited companies.

Companies have a separate legal identity from that of the individuals concerned, but it is the directors who are responsible for ensuring the company acts correctly. By forming a company you can separate your own assets from the business assets, but this separation is conditional upon 'responsible business behaviour'. Move outside of responsible behaviour and the 'shield' of the company no longer protects a director.

Directors' duties

A director also has to cope with some technical, more detailed requirements, for example sending in the accounts to Companies House, appointing an auditor if required, holding regular board meetings and keeping shareholders informed. A director is expected, and required in law, to understand the significance of the balance sheet, profit-and-loss account and cash flow statement, which is more onerous than just signing them.

A director's duties, responsibilities and potential liabilities include:

- To act in good faith in the interests of the company. This includes carrying out duties diligently and honestly.
- Not to carry on the business of the company with intent to defraud creditors or for any fraudulent purpose.

- Not knowingly to allow the company to trade while insolvent ('wrongful trading'). Directors who do so may have to pay for the debts incurred by the company while insolvent.
- Not to deceive shareholders.
- To have a regard for the interests of employees in general.
- To comply with the requirements of the Companies Acts, such as providing what is needed in accounting records or filing accounts.

The Companies Act 2006

The behaviour of companies and their officers is governed by the Companies Acts, a patchwork of legislation started in the Victorian era with the Joint Stock Companies Act of 1844, the Limited Liability Act of 1855 and scores of further pieces of legislation in 1967, 1980 and 1981 that were eventually consolidated into a single act, the Companies Act 1985. That act was itself added to in the decades that followed, but it became apparent that a legislative framework that sought to regulate the affairs of a mere 65,000 companies in 1914 and 200,000 in 1945 was not fit for purpose in governing the affairs of over 1 million companies and their 3 million directors.

For seven years the entirety of company laws was reworked into a single act, the Companies Act 2006, which received royal assent on 8 November 2006. By sweeping away some of the more complex old procedures and introducing new responsibilities for directors and auditors, the key themes of the Act are to make it simpler to set up and run companies, improve shareholder relations and give UK companies a competitive advantage over companies in other countries.

The Act is the longest piece of parliamentary legislation ever introduced, running to some 1,300 sections, all of which come into force by March 2009. This new Act introduces a statutory statement of directors' general duties to provide greater clarity on what is expected of directors, in particular that their general duties are owed to the company, and a director has a duty to promote the success of the company for the success of its members as a whole, putting the long-term interest of the company's shareholders ahead of any other interest. If they do not, they will be acting in breach of their duty to the company.

You can read the key points of the Act on the Companies House website (http://www.companieshouse.gov.uk/companiesAct/podcastArchive.shtml), and at this link you can hear a summary podcast.

Holding board meetings

Board meetings have to be held sufficiently regularly to allow the directors to 'discharge their duties effectively'. On average the boards of public companies meet eight to nine times a year and smaller companies as little as once a quarter. The purposes of board meetings are to take major decisions and to keep everyone informed of events affecting business performance. Having regular board meetings ensures that important matters are properly considered and the various views and outcomes are recorded. Guidelines for successful board meetings are:

- Have as small a number of directors as possible, bearing in mind the size of the business. The amount of useful work a board can do is in inverse proportion to its size.
- Hold meetings regularly and set a timetable a year ahead, updated at the half-year. This is vital if there are non-executive directors.
- Have an agenda and stick to it. Start with the minutes of the previous meeting, get them accepted, move through the agenda and finish with any other business (AOB), also confirming the date and venue for the next meeting.
- Take and circulate minutes of the meeting.
- Have a board chairman, whose role is to keep the board meeting on track.

Appointing a company secretary

Private companies need only one director, provided someone else is appointed as company secretary. Public companies need at least two directors. A director can be a company secretary, but needs to understand that the roles are different. The secretary of a public company must also hold certain qualifications, although this is not the case with private companies. A company secretary has certain administrative functions within the company and may be criminally liable for defaults committed by the company, such as failing to file accounts on time or not notifying Companies House of any change in the details of the company's directors.

A company secretary's responsibilities include:

- arranging board meetings and keeping and circulating the minutes;
- maintaining the statutory registers on directors, shareholders, debentures and loans;

- ensuring that statutory forms and annual returns are filed promptly;
- making out a statement of the company's affairs in the event of it having to be wound up;
- supplying copies of the accounts to shareholders, the bank and all interested parties;
- having custody of the company seal, used to legalize communications from the company.

Companies House (www.companieshouse.gov.uk > Guidance booklets > Directors and secretaries guide) has a comprehensive guide to secretaries' (and directors') duties and the 200 or so forms they may have to file at Companies House.

Taking on auditors

Small companies with a turnover of not more than £5.6 million and a balance sheet total of not more than £2.8 million don't need to have an audit, though any business with outside shareholders will almost certainly be expected to have one.

The audit is the company equivalent of an MOT. The purpose of the audit, which is carried out annually, is to make sure the company has produced its accounts using the prevailing accounting standards and principles and that the figures give a 'true and fair' representation of the company's financial position. In practice in a small company the auditor will rely on the directors supplying correct information and not deliberately concealing or misrepresenting information. You can also expect an auditor to give an opinion about the dependability and appropriateness of the company's accounting methods and systems.

The directors appoint auditors for the first trading year. Once the auditors have audited the company's accounts, the accounts are presented to the shareholders by the directors. The shareholders can then decide to reappoint the auditors, or appoint a different auditor, to hold office until the next accounts are presented and audited – and so on each year.

Auditors have to be members of the major professional accounting bodies. Generally, cost will be crucial factor for a private business in appointing an auditor, unless they are looking specifically to create a degree of external respectability, for example if they are preparing to go public or raise large sums of new capital. You can keep track of who's who in the auditing world through *Accountancy Age* (www.accountancyage.com/resource/top50), which lists the major audit firms in rank order each year.

Wrongful trading and other misdemeanours

There are three types of activities that directors need to steer clear of if they don't want to join the thousand or so directors who are disqualified and fined each year or the rather smaller number who end up at Her Majesty's pleasure for up to seven years or more. In addition you can be made personally liable for the debts and liabilities of any company in which you are involved.

Disqualification means that not only can you not run a company but if you issue your orders through others, having them act as directors in your place, you will leave them personally liable themselves. You will also be in breach of a disqualification order, which can in turn lead to imprisonment and fines.

The three types of activity are:

- Trading whilst insolvent, which occurs when your liabilities exceed your assets. At this point the shareholders' equity in the business has effectively ceased to exist and, when shareholders' equity is negative, directors are personally at risk and owe a duty of care to creditors – not shareholders. If you find yourself even approaching this area you need the prompt advice of an insolvency practitioner. Directors who act properly will not be penalized and will live to fight another day.
- Wrongful trading, which can apply if, after a company goes into insolvent liquidation, the liquidator believes that the directors (or those acting as such) ought to have concluded earlier that the company had no realistic chance of survival. In these circumstances the courts can remove the shelter of limited liability and make directors personally liable for the company's debts.
- Fraudulent trading, which is rather more serious than wrongful trading. Here the proposition is that the directors were knowingly party to fraud on their creditors. The full shelter of limited liability can be removed in these circumstances.

Dealing with business failure

Failure is an unfortunate fact of business life. Over 400,000 businesses close down each year in the United Kingdom alone. Certainly not all are financial disasters, but as companies a number of formalities have to be gone through. These are the main options for closing down a company:

- Voluntary arrangements were brought into being by the Insolvency Act 1986. Until then it was not possible for a debtor to make a legally binding compromise with all his or her creditors. Any single creditor could scupper the plans. Now a debtor can make a proposal to his or her creditors to pay all or part of the debts over a period of time. The mechanics are simple. The debtor applies to the court for an interim order stating that he or she intends to make a proposal, naming a qualified insolvency practitioner who will be advising him or her. The position is then frozen, preventing bankruptcy proceedings until the insolvency practitioner reports back to the court. A creditors' meeting will be called notifying all creditors and, if the proposal is approved by more than 75 per cent by value of the creditors' meeting, it will be binding on all creditors.
- Receivership occurs when a borrower (a company) fails to meet its obligations to a mortgagee. The most usual scenario is where a company gives a charge over assets to its bankers. This in turn allows the banker to advance funds to the company. In these circumstances, if the company fails to meet its obligations to its bankers, for example by not repaying money when due, then the bank can appoint a receiver. The receiver has wide powers to step in and run the business or sell off its assets for the benefit of the person who appointed him or her. The existing directors' authority will be suspended, and existing contracts with the company only have to be carried out by the receiver if he or she believes it worthwhile to do so. Money generated by the receiver first goes to paying the costs of selling assets (auctioneers' fees) and then to paying the receiver's own fees. Only then will the person appointing the receiver get his or her debt paid. Once that too has been discharged, others further down the pecking order, such as preferential debts, may get paid.
- Winding up and liquidation can be imposed on a limited company if it is considered to be unable to pay its debts and a creditor leaves a demand for a debt of £750 or more, in a certain prescribed form, at its registered office and that debt is not paid within 21 days. Once this position is reached an application can be made for the company to be wound up. The company itself can ask to be wound up, as can any creditor, or in some circumstances various government officials can so ask. Before a winding-up order is made the court appoints a provisional liquidator – always called 'the official receiver'. Once the winding-up order is made, all court proceedings against the company are stopped, all employees' contracts are terminated and its directors are dismissed. The liquidator's job is to get in the company's assets and pay off the creditors.

- Administration is a way to help companies in serious financial difficulties to trade their way back to financial health. The thinking here is similar to that behind voluntary arrangements, although administration usually involves much more substantial sums. While in administration the company is protected from its creditors while an approved rescue plan is implemented. Administration orders will be made only where the court is satisfied that the company has cash available from either shareholders or lenders to finance the rescue plan.

Non-executive directors

Despite the comforting sound of the prefix in this title, non-executive directors carry all the responsibilities of full-time directors but are rarely close enough to the business to know exactly what the true financial position is. Big companies like to have them, usually to chair the remuneration committee that determines board salaries and bonuses and to provide further safeguards for shareholders. For small companies sometimes, having a heavyweight outsider can lend extra credibility to a business proposition.

Organizations such as Venture Investment Partners (www.ventureip.co.uk) and the Independent Director Initiative (www.independentdirector.co.uk), a joint venture between Ernst & Young and the Institute of Directors, help in finding suitable non-executive directors for private businesses. Big businesses tend to recruit from within their own network of recently retired directors of major quoted businesses.

Index

Index of advertisers